★ RALPH NADER ★

Presents

PRACTICING DEMOCRACY

A Guide to Student Action

★ RALPH NADER ★
Presents

PRACTICING DEMOCRACY

A Guide to Student Action

★ KATHERINE ISAAC ★

St. Martin's Press, New York

Library of Congress Catalog Number: 94-67003

Manufactured in the United States of America.

9 8 7 6 5
f e d c b

For information, write:
St. Martin's Press, Inc.
175 Fifth Avenue
New York, NY 10010

ISBN 0-312-10789-7

CONTENTS

PREFACE

This book is built on the premise that a healthy democracy requires not only the *right* to participate in the political system, but that its citizens constantly exercise and expand those rights and opportunities. This exercise of democracy involves far more than voting, paying taxes and serving on jury duty; rather, it requires that citizens daily engage in debate, weigh alternatives, and negotiate conflict and controversy to safeguard and expand democracy's rights and freedoms. The grand movements against slavery and for civil rights and workers' rights testify to the power of citizen participation throughout U.S. history. Citizens today, such as those working to halt the consequences of toxic pollution on human health and the environment, continue these traditions by working for a more just society.

Practicing Democracy offers students an overview of the tools and techniques available to citizens wishing to engage in the democratic process. These techniques, including lobbying legislation, waging strikes for workplace rights, and conducting demonstrations and boycotts against unfair corporate practices, are the vehicles through which citizens, as individuals or in groups, can make their voices heard.

The essays by Senator Paul Wellstone, former Republican National Committee chairperson Richard Bond and consumer advocate Ralph Nader offer students three very different perspectives on what it means to become involved in the political process. Wellstone shares his journey from political science professor to U.S. senator via his unique electoral campaign that incorporated his experience as a grassroots organizer; Richard Bond offers insight into his participation in electoral politics; and Ralph Nader shows how students as a class have a unique opportunity to make a significant impact on society.

Whatever the issues or causes that they favor, this book aims to leave students with both the inspiration and the skills to practice democracy.

FOREWORD

On the Importance of Citizen Activism

By U.S. Senator Paul Wellstone (D.-Minn.);
former professor of political science at Carleton College

BACKGROUND: MY JOURNEY FROM THE CAMPUS TO THE U.S. SENATE

For more than twenty years as a college political science teacher I emphasized the centrality of citizen activism. The core principle I imparted was that full participation in our democracy is an essential aspect of citizenship and is crucial for the success of our democracy.

As the son of a Russian Jewish immigrant who fled persecution, it is not surprising that my core ethic is a commitment to participatory democracy—a commitment to improve the lives of people.

My teaching methodology flowed from this commitment to social responsibility. Instead of requiring rote learning, I urged my students to locate themselves personally in relation to the important issues we were studying. Instead of asking students, "What did the book say?" I asked, "What did the book mean to you?"

By teaching with this commitment to social responsibility and action, my purpose was to lead my students toward analysis, understanding, and personal application. In short, I taught my students to develop the conceptual tools necessary to understand our very complicated world. From this understanding, I wanted my students to evaluate different courses of action available for social change. And after evaluating a variety of courses of action, I hoped they would commit themselves to action based on powerfully held beliefs. The ethic was and is that we all must work for what we believe in—or, as I told my students, we cannot separate the lives we live from the words we speak.

I applied the same standard to myself. I came from North Carolina, where I witnessed how the civil rights movement was able to change the United States for the better. With this formative experience, I could not be a dispassionate researcher, writer, or teacher. Instead, for twenty years I taught, wrote, and participated in community organizing.

By the late 1980s, I found myself in strong disagreement with the policies of Republican presidents Ronald Reagan and George Bush. I believed that they were reversing fifty years of social policy and hard-won battles for social justice and economic fairness. I also was increasingly indignant at the timidity of the Democrats. Rather than standing up as a clear voice for justice and economic empowerment, too many Democrats were becoming adjunct members of the Republican party. Following the standards laid out for my students, I decided that the only credible course of action open to me was to become involved in electoral politics.

ix

Race for the U.S. Senate

To the surprise of most, I was the only challenger in 1990 to defeat an incumbent senator. I believe there are three reasons why we won:

1. Progressive issues: My campaign was unabashedly progressive on the issues while being populist in style. People in Minnesota had no doubts about where I stood on the defining issues of our day: choice, civil rights, economic empowerment, jobs, health-care reform, educational excellence, and environmental priorities. People also knew that my populist tradition grew out of their tradition—I traveled the state in a green school bus, stopping in cafés to listen to the stories of working men and women, trying to understand their needs and dreams.

2. Creative TV ads: With so little money, we could not wage a normal television campaign. While our opponent outspent us seven to one, we countered with funny, creative ads that were developed by one of my former students. Instead of resorting to attack ads to tarnish and enrage, our ads managed to get people to smile about politics—a victory in itself.

3. Effective volunteers and get-out-the-vote calls: Most important, my campaign effectively merged grassroots and community organizing by exciting and empowering thousands of individuals from around the state. No one—no political pundit or analyst—anticipated the power of active citizens coming together throughout the campaign. No one anticipated the effect volunteers would have during the last days of the campaign. In the final four days, untold numbers of volunteers made 700,000 get-out-the-vote calls. In the end, all the house parties, the café and school stops, and the commitment to make a difference came together—and we won.

To keep that stirring example of citizen involvement alive, key supporters and democratic activists have formed the Wellstone Alliance to ensure that the 1990 victory was not the victory of just one person. Through the Alliance, we can transfer the skills we learned, we can train campaign managers, and we can encourage and support people to run for political office on all levels, from the local school board and city council to the U.S. Senate.

Looking to the Future

As I look at the decade of the 90s, I am convinced that citizen action and social change will be the decade's defining politics. I believe that there will be three critical ingredients: programs, organizing, and electoral campaigns.

1. We must develop programs and policies because without them we would be a movement without direction. The programs that we articulate and defend should be credible alternatives to the retrograde policies of the 1980s. Indeed, it is incumbent on us to advo-

cate particular policy alternatives that speak directly to people's lives, lest we be intellectually dishonest by simply opposing and criticizing other programs.

2. We must continue our extensive organizing. Programs and policy alternatives are not enough. Without grassroots organizing, we will have a program without a constituency. It is the people at the grassroots level who fight for changes that are important to all of us.

3. Finally, we will continue encouraging people to run for elective office because electoral politics is the main way we contest for power in our country.

CONCLUSION: CITIZEN ACTIVISM AND THE POLITICS OF ANGER

We are living through a volatile, turbulent time in our political history. Indeed, the politics of anger has become a central dynamic in our political discussion.

This anger can take several paths. The citizenry could become more disengaged and more cynical, joining in an across-the-board bashing of politicians and the political process and further denigrating the notion of public service. If this is the path people take, it will only lead to a further decline in our democracy.

Even worse, this politics of anger could spiral down to become fertile ground for the politics of hatred. During hard economic times, without empowering solutions, explanations, and positive citizen action, people's anger can easily be manipulated by demagogues and hatemongers.

However, that same anger could cause people to become more engaged and energized. People could decide that the only way something good in politics will be accomplished is if they take control and become their own leaders. If the anger causes more engagement and accountability, then our country is on the threshold of a new era of citizen participation, and we will witness a rebirth of democracy.

What will happen depends on whether we fulfill the promise of citizen action, which is premised on the belief that each person can be a leader in his or her community.

And that's where students come in. This book is important because it presents you with an opportunity to look at the political world. It allows you to develop your analytical abilities and affords you a chance to see where your talents can contribute to social change. It offers you the same challenge of political involvement that I sought for my students.

In closing, I would like to say a word about Ralph Nader. For years, Ralph Nader and Public Citizen have been presenting opportunities for citizens to develop their skills and become involved to improve the lives of people. He and his organization have been developing policy alternatives and have been at the forefront of social activism and change. Few have done more to merge grassroots activism, policy alternatives, and electoral involvement than he. I'm honored to be writing this foreword at his invitation.

FOREWORD

My Entry into Politics

By Richard N. Bond, former Chairman,
Republican National Committee

My fascination with politics began when I was ten years old. My parents permitted me to stay up late and watch the 1960 Republican and Democratic presidential nominating conventions. Later that year, on a blustery fall afternoon, I stood for hours to catch a glimpse of John Kennedy as his motorcade passed slowly through my hometown on Long Island.

More than thirty years later I realized one of my life's ambitions and stood before a national audience and gavelled open the Republican National Convention as Chairman of the Republican party. Over the twelve years of the Reagan and Bush presidencies, I rode in numerous motorcades and watched people straining to glimpse their nation's leader— much as I had done as a boy.

Politics is a unique profession. It can be uplifting and fulfilling, while at the same time, disappointing and disheartening. Some might say that, at its simplest, politics is about winning and losing. However, that is only part of the story. Every year thousands of men and women enter politics. The reasons why they run for office or work in campaigns are as different as the positions for which they compete.

As a child, I was first drawn to the excitement and the spectacle of politics. However, as I got older, I was motivated by more serious purposes. Government is the primary agent of change in America. "Having a voice" in government is important to most people. Peaceful change through the political process has brought free speech to millions of people in Eastern Europe and the former Soviet Union. Unfortunately, many Americans sometimes take their First Amendment right for granted. Involvement in politics gives your voice weight and influence on issues that you care about - from education and the environment to the economy and foreign affairs. Participation in campaigns, politics, and, ultimately, government, gives you a say in your own personal future and in the future of your friends, family, neighborhood, and nation.

My major attraction in politics has been to campaigns and the Republican party. In high school I rang doorbells and put up yard signs for local candidates. In college I debated the issue of the Vietnam War and went door to door for Mayor John Lindsay of New York City. After graduation, I worked in the Nassau County government, and I met George Bush, who was then the Republican party's national chairman.

At the time, Mr. Bush was speaking at our annual fund raiser. The Watergate scandal, which ultimately ended the presidency of Richard Nixon, was in full force. Millions of voters felt let down by Nixon and alienated from the Republican party. Bush had the difficult job of defending the president while distancing the Republican party from a scandal in which it had no part. His forceful performance on behalf of President Nixon and his broader message about Republican principles made a lasting impression. He presented the Republican party as a worthy cause, dedicated to the proposition that the government that governs least governs best. I saw a disconnection between national leaders who governed without regard for fiscal responsibility and the taxpayers who provided the tax revenues. I saw a lack of accountability and wanted to help change the system and make leaders more responsive to citizens.

I left my job in county government and began to work on political campaigns—as a state representative, a county executive, and then a lieutenant governor. For almost two decades, I held a series of related jobs: campaign manager, field operative for the Republican National Committee, congressional press secretary, presidential campaign political director, and White House aide. Then, nineteen years from the time that I first met George Bush, I succeeded him as chairman of the Republican National Committee.

As party leader, I found echoes of what I had encountered a decade and a half earlier. Ironically, it was now President Bush who needed a strong defense from a Republican party chairman. His popularity had plummeted, the media were hostile, and Democrats (including Bill Clinton) were lined up to run against him. He was even facing a primary challenge from within his own party, as Republicans felt let down by Bush's economic policies and were drifting away from his banner. So it happened that I was to defend the former party chairman who had, in his own defense of a beleaguered president, inspired me to pursue a career in politics.

Even though Bush lost the presidency, the Republican party emerged intact. It gained seats in the House of Representatives (the only time in the century that has happened when the party's president was defeated), broke even in the Senate, and made substantial gains on the state legislative level. As is customary in the face of a presidential defeat, I stepped down as party leader. I did so with my love for politics intact, and with an eye toward reclaiming the White House in the next election.

My personal odyssey from a grassroots volunteer as a high school student to the leader of one of our nation's two political parties is testimony to the virtue of involvement. Every door is open in politics—to men, women, young, old, minorities, the disabled, the disadvantaged. Politics asks only that you volunteer your time and make your voice heard. After that, your imagination will be your only boundary.

INTRODUCTION

By Ralph Nader

Our society is reaching the point where, the more citizens default on solving major pressing problems, the bigger the penalties. Fifty years ago if citizens did not reduce, reuse, and recycle, they found another dump. Now, if something is not done, we end up with a polluting incinerator a few miles away and with trucks and railway cars carrying hazardous waste through communities. Different responses—and different consequences—result from citizen inactivity or indifference. Whether it is street crime, poverty, business abuses, or toxic pollution, there is an inescapable impact on the quality of community life. Citizens working to build and rebuild movements of reconstruction and redress are faced with ever more complex and time-absorbing demands. These demands on our practice of citizenship grow with the expansion of a complex, interdependent society. Both our supply and quality of citizenship, equipped with modern democratic tools, must keep up.

This need logically brings us to our schools and universities, where there is inadequate emphasis on learning the civic skills needed to study, evaluate, and then improve society. Our educational institutions, in large part, are neglecting an important mission. Students rarely have the opportunity to study the phenomenon known as corporate crime even though it is widespread in the United States. Engineering or physics courses do not encourage students to merge theory and practice, for example, by applying what they have learned to a particular issue in the community. A pollution exposure, a water purification challenge, or a sewage-system problem could provide a clinical opportunity for students to contribute to their community. Almost every skill and academic discipline can find a ready use in the complex drive for social change and in the protection and advancement of people and rights in our society.

Students are citizens, they are buyers, they are or will be taxpayers. Yet they are not taught and encouraged to develop the citizenship skills can improve their performance in these roles.
This results in a shameful waste of human potential and in millions of students who lack civic self-confidence. Given the opportunity, many students could become effective advocates for democratic solutions to our society's problems.

Despite media reports to the contrary, students today still have the basic generic idealism or desire for a better society. A report from People for the American Way concluded that students "are not, by and large, selfish or apathetic; they seem instead to be well-meaning people with weak civic skills." Provided with those skills and a chance to practice them, students can learn and grow. They can start to be judged by what they do, rather than by their looks or their socioeconomic status. But student efforts face a number of obstacles. Many students are not involved in civic activity because of personal anxieties, concerns, and problems. They need encouragement in their shift to different commitments and priorities; they need a larger frame of reference. Involvement in important civic purposes such as environmental health, a just government, or minority rights can bring deep and lasting rewards. Work with others to address larger problems in society can help dissolve or reduce these personal perplexities.

Another hurdle is that most students do not look at themselves as a unique group. The higher education community in the United States contains thirteen million community college, undergraduate, and graduate students. Yet students who are thirteen million strong do not have even one weekly national television program that addresses what they are doing and thinking about outside the athletic arena. Because they do not consider themselves as a distinct class in the population, engaged in interesting and important activities on campus, there is little self-realization that students need, deserve, and can demand such a program. There are, already, engineering students who are further developing solar energy and new kinds of automotive engines. Students are artists, poets, activists. These pursuits deserve the kind of media and public attention now paid to the eccentric rites of spring.

Further, students underestimate their own power. If intimidated by university trustees who deny their democratic or educational rights, they must look for ways to challenge the trustees, uncover their conflicts of interest, and appeal for alumni and community support. They should realize they can become the statewide experts on an issue, as evidenced by student Jill Siegel, who is profiled in this book. They should realize that collectively they can put together a successful information or legislative campaign. Such activities take time, planning, and skill, but they can be accomplished. Some people forget that students have been key organizers or backers of the major social movements of the past three decades: the civil rights movement, the anti-apartheid campaign, and the environmental and antinuclear movements. Indeed throughout U.S. history, it is citizens, from minorities of one to mass movements, who in a thousand ways over two hundred years, have rescued their country from shame, error, cruelty, and decline.

To overcome obstacles to greater civic experience, students need to appreciate their present assets. They are near the peak of their idealism. With their access to libraries, laboratories, and faculty, they have a proximity to technical information that is highly desirable in any kind of public policy struggle. Students can double-track their scholarly or academic work with their civic action. For instance, in political science courses, students can profile members of Congress or agency heads and disseminate what they learn through the media. In chemistry and biology courses, students can test drinking water, air samples, and food contamination. They can apply their knowledge to political action.

A steel worker is going to have trouble going to the steel mill, putting in a day's work, and fighting pollution at the same time. The worker might be fired for being an advocate. Students are much freer, which is another asset that they hold. They are at an age and in a situation more conducive to assuming bold steps, to speaking out in protest. The invisible chains are not so tight—students have the time, energy, idealism, and resources to act on the movements of today and of the future.

Finally, students have their own local media—newspapers and radio stations—and their own gathering halls in which to meet and rally for their causes. Most citizens do not have access to comparable facilities in their daily environments. What remains is for students to develop a frame of reference and sound directions for their energies.

Students need to compare their rights with the rights of citizens in some other countries who cannot speak out, protest, demand better working conditions, stop police brutality, or participate in democratic elections. There are not many countries in the world where civic work can be carried forward as it can in the United States, under the blessing of our Constitution and the active citizens who give its words both foundation and life. Today, students in other countries are on the ramparts, risking their lives to get a fraction of the rights that students in the United States have and too often do not use.

The hard realization is that each of us is both a private citizen and a public citizen. Most students want a good station in life, a good income, a home, a car, and a vacation cottage. That's being a private citizen. Usually, people are adequately motivated in the private area. What we need is a special effort in the public citizen area. That effort can be endlessly rewarding. Civic participation is a formula for human happiness, both private and public. It is more than a slogan to be intoned or even a duty to be self-imposed; it is a delight to be savored as the essential quality of life that makes democracy an authentic reality. It is a pleasure for students to fulfill themselves by applying the principles of justice in a democratic, community forum—complete with debate, dialogue, advocacy, assertion, and implementation. They see that, as some battles are lost, others are won. They learn to keep going, and that, from loss and adversity come the positive benefits of becoming more strategically astute and more determined.

This experience is reflected in the current history of student-funded and student-directed public interest research groups (PIRGs), with their full-time staffs operating in many states to improve their communities and train students to become sustainable citizens long after graduation.

In a nation characterized by its progressive development of humane ideals, what has begun as a sensitive effort by a few volunteers has often matured into more deeply rooted structures that have defended and implemented a set of enlightened values on a daily basis. Fire fighting, libraries, soil conservation programs, women's right to vote, worker safety, civil rights, consumer rights, legal services for the poor, feeding programs for the hungry, laws protecting the many against the few, educational institutions and services—these are a small sample of social improvements stimulated into being by people who had broader definitions of human values or citizen work than their contemporary cultures initially recognized.

Some of America's students are already among our active citizens. They have learned to combine their energy, academic knowledge, and organizational skills with their dedication to the community around them. They are preparing themselves for life and for work as citizen/activists— the true legacy of a democratic society.

To those students who have yet to make a commitment to civic life: Why not resolve to make a mark on your school and community *before* you leave college, so that those who come after you will benefit? Do not simply coast and accept what has been given by those who have gone before you. Try to change and improve, expand, and enliven the atmosphere, the environment, the courses, and the curriculum. Your sense of contributing to a legacy, of having a longer view, and of benefiting more than yourself will be very valuable to you throughout your life. May the following pages find their uses in the minds and hearts of citizens eager to build a more just, sustainable, and happy world.

GETTING STARTED

"This country has more problems than it should tolerate and more solutions than it uses," writes Ralph Nader in the introduction to *Action for a Change: A Student's Manual for Public Interest Organizing.*[1] You will not need to look far on your university campus or in your community for problems that students and citizens can help solve. Instead of complaining that no one is doing anything, choose one problem or issue and get started. When setting long-range goals, try to imagine a model university, neighborhood, or world. Then think of concrete ways to work toward those goals. Offer concrete solutions that attack the root of the problem.

Narrow down an issue to small goals attainable in a relatively brief period of time. For example, if you are concerned about the environment, start by initiating a campus recycling drive. Once you have learned more about recycling and solid-waste issues, promote recycling in the community and then lobby for local, state, and federal solid waste policies that reflect your concerns.

Once you have chosen an issue and goals, decide whether to address the issue as an individual, join an organization that works on that issue, or start your own group. Then plan a strategy and choose tactics to help you reach your goals.

Discussed here are some of the many tactics and techniques that citizens have used throughout U.S. history to gain access to decision makers and to resolve community problems. You will not use all or even most of the tactics in one campaign, but wise choices will further your cause.

For example, in 1985, citizens in New York City organized to oppose a proposed garbage incinerator. First, ten thousand New Yorkers marched across the Brooklyn Bridge to show their opposition. The student-run New York Public Interest Research Group (NYPIRG) conducted a study of the environmental, health, and financial consequences of the proposed incinerator. The report, which attracted media attention, offered an alternative in the form of a comprehensive recycling plan. Volunteers went door to door handing out leaflets to let others in the affected community know about the proposal and to urge them to call the mayor to voice their opposition to the proposed incinerator. More than ninety local groups, including student groups from all nine New York City universities, formed a coalition to fight the incinerator. NYPIRG filed a lawsuit, and the permit hearings for the incinerator were put on hold. NYPIRG and other groups lobbied the state legislature for a bill to support recycling.[2] As of August 1993, the coalition had succeeded in preventing the issuance of any new permits and continued to work for a moratorium on incineration.

INDIVIDUAL ACTION

Many of the techniques used to bring about change are most effective when carried out by groups of people, but individuals can use many tactics successfully. Individuals can take action by distributing pamphlets; attending and speaking at public meetings; gathering signatures for petitions; writing letters, making telephone calls, or sending telegrams to government officials, the media, and businesses; boycotting products or businesses; and blowing the whistle on unsafe, illegal, or unethical practices.

Pamphleteering

One citizen who practices the philosophy that one person can make a difference is Charles L. Smith of Berkeley, California, who educates the public by disseminating information through pamphlets. Smith writes, "Pamphleteering is the personal use of the freedoms of speech and press. . . . It is an excellent system for introducing new ideas in an open society." He notes that "pamphleteering has historically been used by persons who have sought to bring about change of intolerable situations," including Sam Adams, Thomas Paine, and Margaret Sanger.[3]

Smith, who started pamphleteering in 1949, concentrates on issues that are not debated or discussed widely. He reads newspapers, magazines, and journals, clipping articles about the many topics in which he is interested, such as parking and transportation problems, prison reform, and drinking water quality. Acting as an individual, Smith passes on to the citizens of Berkeley and surrounding communities information that they are otherwise unlikely to receive. For example, when a nuclear power plant was proposed for Bodega Bay, California, in 1963, Smith took action by standing on a street corner wearing a sign that read "Bodega: 'Boom' or Bust?" and handing out informative flyers about the plant's economic and safety problems.[4]

Smith recommends that a pamphleteer create a flyer that is "authoritative, readable, reasonable, logical, concise and in general presentable and acceptable." The flyer should not libel any person or organization. Next, create "a simple, readable sign (legible at a suitable distance) to be worn or displayed in a manner which predisposes passersby to accept your pamphlet." Smith gives his pamphlets only to people who demonstrate curiosity or acceptance, and hence few people discard them. Smith recommends distributing flyers on a street corner or in other places where many potentially interested people may gather, such as conferences on related issues.[5]

Whistle-blowing

Whistle-blowing—disclosing information about an illegal or dangerous action, usually in the workplace—is another form of individual action.[6] One example of a whistle-blower is Linda Porter who received the 1991 Cavallo Prize for Moral Courage, which is awarded to individuals who "have chosen to speak out when it would have been far easier to have remained silent." Porter, an employee of Brown and Root, Inc., a construction contractor at the Comanche Peak nuclear power plant in Texas, blew the whistle on worker health and safety violations she experienced at the plant.[7]

Porter began work at the plant in 1984. Her job was "to apply, strip, and replace heavy paint coating on the plant structures." Although her employer trained her in occupational safety, when Porter began to raise questions about the safety of crumbling concrete supports, "her concerns were met with ridicule," and "she and her crew were assigned to the dirtiest and most difficult jobs." Eventually, Porter was demoted and then fired. Within months, however, the company hired her back.

In 1987, Porter discovered that the coatings that she and other workers routinely used contained asbestos as well as several chemicals rated by government agencies as among the most dangerous for workers and the environment. Not only Comanche Peak employees but also the entire community was at risk because the plant dumped extra containers of coating into unlined pits not far from a recreational reservoir near the plant.

Although Porter notified management of her findings and then reported them to the Nuclear Regulatory Commission and the Occupational Safety and Health Administration, Brown and Root continued its intimidation tactics against Porter. The company forced Porter and her crew to test the asbestos content of coatings applied to the walls of one room in the plant by sanding the coatings from the walls. The respirator Porter used to protect herself from the dust failed, and she ingested large amounts of the dust through her nose and throat. Porter continued to express safety concerns and was fired again.

The asbestos testing left Porter with a myriad of health problems. Despite her failing health, Porter stepped up her efforts to ensure that the plant management dealt with safety problems. She contacted the Government Accountability Project (GAP), a Washington, D.C.-based organization that provides legal assistance to "concerned citizens who witness dangerous, illegal, or environmentally unsound practices in their workplaces and communities and choose to 'blow the whistle.'" GAP is working with local groups in Texas "to ensure that the toxic chemicals are removed from unsafe landfills near the plant."

As Porter continues her fight, she says, "What I'm seeking is for industry to understand that we're not going to be throwaway workers, and I want a message sent to regulators that they're not supposed to let this happen."[8]

Citizen groups lobbied Congress for legislation to protect whistle-blowers, who often fear that coming forward will cost them their job or their personal safety. Congress passed the Whistle-blower Protection Act in 1989 which strengthens the government employees' code of ethics and offers some protections to federal government whistle-blowers.[9]

FORMING A CITIZEN GROUP AND RECRUITING SUPPORTERS

Individuals may find that joining with other people is more effective than working alone. Students may wish to start a new university-based organization, join an existing group or club, or form a coalition of existing groups to work on a particular issue.

"There are several reasons why it is worth taking the time to organize a citizen action group," writes Mark Green and colleagues in *Who Runs Congress?* "A group can commit more energy and resources than even the most dedicated individual. A group is more likely to have resources and endurance to carry a seemingly interminable project through to completion."[10]

A local group may want to affiliate with a national group or form a coalition with like-minded groups, but if you decide to start a new group, advise Stephen Newman and Nancy Kramer in *Getting What You Deserve*, "There is no sure-fire, clear-cut blueprint for success; the goals, background and personalities of the founders will all determine the direction."[11]

Newman and Kramer instead offer the following tips: visit other groups to ask for advice and support; hold a meeting as soon as you have several people who are really interested in participating, not just joining. Start with a specific agenda for the meeting, but let others contribute their ideas and suggestions; begin with one or two activities to avoid exhausting the group's energy; assign specific tasks to people, sharing responsibility and glory; and set small, reachable goals.

Types of Citizen Groups

Three common types of citizen groups are the citizen lobby, the citizen coalition, and the community organization.[12]

Typically, a citizen lobby works to influence policy through a central office in the state capital or Washington and a network of citizens around the state or country ready to make phone calls, write letters, send telegrams, and join together for demonstrations, visits to legislators, and other actions at the capital.[13]

A coalition is a group of organizations working to pursue common interests. Coalitions show the backing of a wide variety of groups on a particular issue. And according to Marc Caplan in *A Citizens' Guide to Lobbying*, coalitions "pool the skills and resources of the groups involved, greatly increasing the resources that can be brought to bear on the issue."[14] One example of a coalition is the Citizen/Labor Energy Coalition, formed in 1977 by labor unions and citizen and environmental groups to work on energy issues by "developing policies that provide jobs, conservation, and price protection."[15] Often coalitions form around a specific issue and disband when the issue is resolved.

Community organizing generally refers to people with common problems joining together to solve those problems and to exercise power in the decisions that affect their lives. A community can be your class, school, neighborhood, or town. Community organizer Lee Staples writes, "To solve problems, people need to get some control over the concrete circumstances of everyday life. Organizing seeks to do this. . . . When people join together and organize, they increase their ability to get things done."[16]

Experienced organizers work to help people in communities learn the strength of their power and learn to participate in decision-making processes. When people are organized, they are always a factor in the decisions that employers, government officials, and landlords make every day, and they do not need to depend only on a friendly lawyer or politician to take care of problems for them.[17]

Organizing has intangible as well as concrete benefits. People work together to make their community a better place to live and achieve a sense of satisfaction. As organizer Si Kahn writes, "People learn something new about themselves. They find dignity in place of mistreatment. They find self-respect instead of a lack of self-confidence. They begin to use more fully the skills and abilities that they possess: to work with other people, to influence, to speak up, to fight back."[18]

Community organizing uses many of the techniques described here. The techniques, however, are part of a long-term strategy to make citizens a permanent fixture in the community decision-making process.

To build community support, organizers go door to door to identify interested people or issues of concern to the community, hold meetings, and speak at community gatherings and religious groups to discuss issues and plan strategies.

One tactic that community organizations use is the accountability session—a meeting with elected officials at which members of the community can tell the official what they want done. Accountability sessions aim to work out agreements with officials at the meeting.[19]

The United States has a long history of community organizing, but Saul Alinsky, who set up the Industrial Areas Foundation in 1940, developed and refined community organizing as a technique and a profession.[20] Alinsky helped communities across the country organize themselves, trained other organizers, and inspired the creation of dozens of new groups. Harry Boyte writes in *The Backyard Revolution*, "Alinsky was extraordinarily creative in developing tactics and strategies for grassroots organizations. . . . He urged tactics full of surprises, irreverence, drama and rapid change."[21]

One organization that built on the Alinsky model is National People's Action (NPA), a Chicago neighborhood group. When NPA discovered that local banks were redlining the neighborhood—systematically refusing to approve loans for residents living within a particular area, regardless of qualifications—they used Alinsky-style tactics to change the banks' practice. Founder Gale Cincotta and her neighbors "disrupted business as usual by staging protests like taking up officers' time opening new accounts, then immediately closing them." Since its founding in 1972, NPA has worked on such issues as housing, banking, energy costs, health care, and military spending.[22] Hundreds of other community organizations, including the Association of Community Organizations for Reform Now (ACORN) and Citizen Action networks, are active across the country.

Recruitment

Once an organization is formed, launch an education program to let the rest of the community know what the group is doing and to recruit members. When asked to join an organization, people naturally will want to know about the group's goals and tactics. Talking with people face to face is the best way to involve them. To recruit members, citizen groups often go door to door (canvass) in the neighborhood affected by an issue, hold house meetings, and speak at meetings of other community groups.[23] To recruit other students at your university, ask to speak to classes or groups, and set up an information table in the cafeteria, the bookstore, or some other high-traffic area. Ask people interested for a small commitment, such as attending a meeting, writing a letter to a legislator, or signing a petition. Once members have been recruited, it is important to put them to work, letting them use their talents effectively to attack the goal from many angles.[24]

House meetings are a simple and effective way to recruit new members. Community organizer Fred Ross developed the house meeting method in the early 1950s when he organized Mexican American farm workers in Tustin, California, to fight segregated schools. Ross was struggling to find a way to bring people together when the farm workers suggested the idea.[25]

Ross asked farm workers who were interested to invite their friends to small meetings at their homes to spread the word about issues and ways to become involved. Ross reached many people through these house meetings and successfully organized a voter registration drive that helped elect school board officials who ended school segregation in the area.[26]

Fred Ross taught the method to Cesar Chavez, founder of the United Farm Workers (UFW). When Chavez and Dolores Huerta, the first vice-president of the UFW, began organizing farm workers, they used the house meeting method. Where other methods failed, through house meetings, says Huerta, "we were able to get together a thousand farm workers who were willing to put their names on the line and start paying their dues."[27]

PUBLIC EDUCATION

Educating others about a particular issue is essential to mobilizing public support, and the methods for doing so are limited only by the imagination. Public education methods include flyers, newsletters, reports, community hearings, and video productions. Many other techniques are also educational; for example, a picket informs the public about a complaint while pressuring its target.

Leaflets, Flyers, Posters, and Bulletin Boards

Distributing leaflets and flyers helps get a message to a large number of people quickly. Flyers are usually a single page with a clear and concise message capable of attracting attention. Distribute flyers where people congregate, including shopping malls and community gatherings; post them on bulletin boards, and place them on car windshields.

Leaflets or flyers are a good way to publicize an event such as a demonstration or a fundraiser, briefly explain a group's views on an issue, and recruit members to a campaign. When publicizing an event, Nancy Brigham, in *How to Do Leaflets, Newsletters and Newspapers,* suggests including the following information on leaflets: place and type of event, date and time, reason why it is important, name of the sponsoring group, person to contact, and a phone number to call. Brigham also recommends that leaflets tackle one issue at a time, be specific, offer solutions when describing problems, and be consistent in style so that people recognize flyers from the organization.[28]

Posters are more permanent announcements of meetings and actions than flyers and keep the issue in the public eye.

A bulletin board is another way to let people know about current issues and activities. Charles Smith points out that "a good, well-operated bulletin board can make a community center into much more than just a gathering point. It can be a constant source of new or individual information."[29]

Clearinghouses

A clearinghouse—a repository for information about specific issues—serves as a network to link individuals and groups with interests in common and to share information. The constituency may be the people of a single neighborhood or community, people or organizations across the country, or international organizations.

Collecting information for a clearinghouse is an ongoing process. People contact clearinghouses looking for up-to-date as well as historical information. Clearinghouse operators organize the information in a filing cabinet or in a computer database and provide information over the phone, by mail, or via computer.

One example of a local clearinghouse is the Berkeley Information Network (BIN). Sponsored by the Berkeley, California, public library, BIN provides community information and referrals at the library and over the telephone. BIN maintains files with information on over 2,500 organizations, agencies, and clubs that serve Berkeley residents.

Newsletters

Newsletters educate and inform less active members of an organization or members who live away from the focus of the group's activities. Newsletters often contain updates on recent group actions, news related to the issues, and opportunities for participation by less active members. Many citizen groups use newsletters to help maintain the solidarity and cohesion of a large organization, as well as to increase participation by members.

Newsletters can do a lot more than simply report a group's activities. Nancy Brigham suggests reporting on important news that affects your readers but is not adequately covered by local newspapers or TV news; covering the lives and activities of "ordinary" people in your neighborhood or town; reporting other groups' activities, as well as how they got started and their motivations and goals; and including a letters page to let readers voice their opinions about the newsletter or other relevant issues. A newsletter can be an important forum for the exchange of information and ideas.[30]

Brigham's book is an excellent guide to both the technical and substantive aspect of publishing a newsletter or newspaper.

Reports and Surveys

Citizen groups use reports and surveys to document evidence that a particular problem exists or is widespread and to offer the groups' solutions for change. A report can alert government officials, the media, and the public to an issue and what can be done about it. Taping a video is another way to document a problem, such as a busy intersection that needs a traffic light.

The United States Public Interest Research Group (U.S. PIRG), the national office of the campus-based PIRGs, studies and reports on the correlation between the voting records of members of Congress and the campaign contributions they accept. When U.S. PIRG compared campaign contributions from nuclear power industry political action committees (PACs) to congressional voting records on issues affecting the nuclear industry, it found "a link between PAC receipts and support of the nuclear industry's positions." According to Gene Karpinski, executive director of U.S. PIRG, "It appears that the real reason for the contributions is to buy access and influence votes."[31] U.S. PIRG uses the PAC studies to advocate campaign finance reform.

Residents living near Love Canal in Niagara Falls, New York, after repeated attempts to convince government officials of the seriousness of residents' health problems related to exposure to toxic chemicals, conducted their own health survey. The Love Canal Homeowners Association surveyed women in the Love Canal area who had become pregnant in 1979. Of the fifteen pregnancies, only one resulted in a healthy baby; four ended in miscarriages, two infants were stillborn, and nine others, including a set of twins, were born with deformities.[32] The survey results were alarming and heightened the urgency in solving the problem.

Speakers' Bureaus

A speakers' bureau is a group of people ready and able to give speeches or conduct workshops on specific issues. The League of Women Voters selects members of its organization to form a speakers' bureau as a way of educating the public about issues of importance. Bureau speakers prepare speeches geared toward different listeners and contact other citizen groups, civic associations, schools, and professional associations to offer their services at meetings and conferences.[33]

Physicians for Social Responsibility (PSR)—an organization of doctors dedicated to the prevention of nuclear war, the redirection of military

spending to health-care programs, and environmental preservation—
operates a speakers' bureau. PSR recruits doctors from its membership to
speak about topics such as the physician's role in preventing war, radio-
active and toxic pollutants, and health-care reform. The PSR speakers'
bureau adds speaking topics as new issues of concern arise; for example,
after the Chernobyl nuclear accident in the Soviet Union in 1986, bureau
speakers addressed the effects of radiation on human health.[34]

Contact local chapters of national organizations working on issues of
interest to ask about leading activists and speakers in your community
and state. Some local newspapers have speakers' bureaus as a service to
the community. See the Resources section at the back of this book for more
information.

Public Hearings, Candidates Nights, and Film or Video Screenings

Although official hearings are held at all levels of government and usually provide some measure of citizen participation, citizen groups often
call their own hearings when the government, workplace, or business
refuses to include citizen points of view. For example, because the National Welfare Rights Organization (NWRO) anticipated that it would not
receive a fair hearing, its held its own hearing at the U.S. Capitol in
November 1970 on a proposed welfare program. Organizers set the hearing two days before scheduled action by the Senate Finance Committee.
Senator Fred Harris, a member of the Finance Committee, was so im-
pressed by the hearing that he voted in favor of the NWRO plan, supply-
ing the vote it needed to pass the committee.[35]

Hearings allow community members to ask questions and voice concerns to public or corporate officials and also can educate, publicize, and
establish an organization as a leading force on the issue. Convincing
potential participants to attend a hearing might be difficult. Yet Kim Bobo
and colleagues, in *Organizing for Social Change*, point out that officials may
find it difficult to explain a refusal to discuss issues with a large number
of constituents.[36]

Other ideas for educating a local community include holding a candidates night to give the community an opportunity to ask candidates
where they stand on certain issues, conducting a teach-in, and holding a
community screening of a film or video that helps explain an issue. See
the Resources section for video ideas.

RESEARCH

Researching an issue helps to identify the source of a problem, develop
workable solutions, and plan tactics for implementing solutions. Research
methods vary widely, but this section covers general background research, right-to-know tools including a detailed guide to using the Freedom of Information Act, and sources of information on elected officials—

9

from voting records to campaign finance. Students can also use the information gathered about elected officials to conduct a public education project by profiling their members of Congress or state legislators.

To research an issue effectively find information from supporting and opposing points of view. Identify who is responsible for causing the problem and who has the authority to change it. Also find out what is not known about a subject—for example, the long-term health effects of a certain pollutant. Keep good records of information sources, including telephone calls, meetings, interviews, and all written sources, and whenever possible, get statements in writing. Clip newspaper and magazine articles related to your issue and keep them in a file.[37]

Background Research

Start at the library. Use newspaper and magazine articles to provide background on an issue and to help you decide where to go next in your research. The *Reader's Guide to Periodical Literature* indexes about 180 popular magazines, but more than 50,000 magazines are published in the United States. Most libraries have specialized indexes for trade and professional journals from many different subjects and fields. Try the *Alternative Press Index* for small political magazines and newsletters. The *Business Periodicals Index* is a good place to look for magazine articles on industry and particular corporations.

Most libraries have a number of directories of corporations, including *Standard and Poor's Register of Executives and Directors, Moody's Manuals,* and *Dun and Bradstreet's Million Dollar Directory*, which list information on major corporations, including corporate officers, members of the boards of directors, financial information, subsidiaries, and dates of annual meetings.

Broadcast news programs are also indexed. *Television News Index and Abstracts* covers the national evening news broadcast by ABC, CBS, and NBC since 1972. *The McNeil-Lehrer Report* is a printed index to transcripts of all of those programs, on microform from 1976 to the present.

Consult the *United States Government Manual* to find out which agency or department of the federal government, if any, has the authority to change the situation, to research past and present policies and laws, and to determine which agencies are responsible for regulating which industries. For local and state issues, call elected officials.

The federal government operates a depository library system that automatically sends the major documents the government publishes—bills, laws, and agency journals and magazines—to the 1,400 participating libraries, including one in each congressional district. More than two-thirds of the states operate a state documents depository system. Copies of major state documents and publications are sent automatically to selected libraries around the state. The local library may have documents that are published locally, such as municipal budgets and committee reports.

Many libraries are beginning to subscribe to some of the thousands of computerized databases, which range from a computerized index to actual newspaper and magazine articles on line. Searching a database for information can save time but is generally expensive—from $35 to several hundred dollars per hour. Some cities and states are computerizing files, which are then available twenty-four hours a day to anyone with a personal computer and a modem.

PeaceNet and EcoNet are nonprofit computer networks run by the Institute for Global Communications that link groups around the world. You can find out what other groups are doing or make an announcement yourself using computer conferencing and electronic mail (E-mail).

Other good sources of information include the local newspaper's files, community publications, and personal contacts with people familiar with similar issues. Use the resources in the back of this book to find citizen groups that work on issues of interest.

The Right to Know

Citizen and labor groups have campaigned for right-to-know provisions to gain access to government and corporate information. Right-to-know provisions make possible citizen access to information such as toxic hazards, bank records, and all types of government records.[38] The Emergency Planning and Community Right to Know Act, the Occupational Safety and Health Administration's hazard communication standard, and the Freedom of Information Act are some of the formal right-to-know tools.

In 1986, Congress passed the Emergency Planning and Community Right to Know Act, which directs the Environmental Protection Agency (EPA) to compile an inventory of all chemical polluters (in 1987, more than eighteen thousand facilities and over seven hundred toxic chemicals) and make that information available to the public.[39] The citizen group OMB Watch publishes a guide to the law.[40] In 1988, the EPA computerized the information, called the Toxic Release Inventory (TRI), through which citizens can find out what companies release what types of chemicals into their communities and in what quantities.[41] Access to the TRI computer database is available through the National Library of Medicine in Bethesda, Maryland.[42] Environmental activists around the country use the information to oppose toxic pollution in their communities.[43]

The Occupational Safety and Health Administration (OSHA) is the federal agency responsible for monitoring and enforcing laws and regulations that govern worker health and safety. OSHA covers only private industry, but some states have set up similar agencies to cover municipal and state workers. Under the right-to-know hazard communication standard, containers of hazardous chemicals must provide an immediate warning to workers, more detailed information on the chemical and its hazards must be made available on a material safety data sheet, and the employer must offer training to ensure that workers understand the labels and know how to handle hazardous substances safely.[44]

The Community Reinvestment Act requires banks to have a public file that describes how the bank plans to serve the community, including making loans to low-income people. Citizen groups often use this information to challenge whether banks are meeting this obligation.

The Freedom of Information Act

To demonstrate the degree of secrecy within federal government agencies, Representative John E. Moss of California held congressional hearings from 1955 to 1966. Moss, as a member of Congress, often found it difficult to convince the executive branch to share information with Congress. As a result of these hearings, Congress enacted the Freedom of Information Act (FOIA) in 1966 to give the public access to information collected and held by the federal government.[45]

The FOIA guarantees the right to request and receive any document, file, or other record—including papers, reports, letters, films, computer tapes, photographs, and sound recordings—in the possession of any agency of the federal government, subject to nine specific exemptions.[46] The FOIA also authorizes information requesters to sue in federal court to force federal agencies to comply with the act.

Many federal agencies quickly found ways to subvert the new law by delaying their responses to requests, charging high fees for searching for and copying records, and interpreting the exemptions to the Act very broadly. Citizen groups lobbied Congress for a stronger law, which was passed in 1974. The FOIA amendments imposed response deadlines, a waiver of search and copying fees for information to be used in the public benefit, and narrower definitions as to what records are exempt from the act (see Table 1).[47]

The FOIA is a powerful tool for citizens monitoring the activities of government or business. Because of it, most government information is available to all who seek it. Citizen groups, journalists, and scholars have used the act to "uncover hundreds of cases of government waste and fraud, unsafe environmental practices, dangerous consumer products, unethical behavior and assorted wrongdoing" such as "the dangerous defects in Firestone 500 steel-belted radial tires and the exploding gas tanks of Ford Pintos."[48]

The FOIA has opened the files of the Federal Bureau of Investigation (FBI), which has a long history of gathering intelligence on the activities of domestic political organizations. Much of this investigative work, particularly under the administration of J. Edgar Hoover, FBI director from 1924 to 1972, was conducted without the knowledge or permission of the president or the attorney general, who are supposed to direct the actions of the agency.[49] Between 1956 and 1971, Hoover conducted counterintelligence programs (COINTELPRO), involving wiretaps and break-ins, against civil rights organizations including the Student Nonviolent Coordinating Committee, anti–Vietnam War groups such as Students for a Democratic Society, the Communist party, the Socialist Workers party, the women's

Table 1

Freedom of Information Act Exemptions

1. National security information
2. Internal agency rules—exempts rules and practices of agency personnel that are "predominantly internal" and where disclosure serves no substantial public interest
3. Information exempted by another federal statute—honors mandatory nondisclosure provisions in other laws, such as laws governing income tax returns and completed Census Bureau forms
4. Trade secrets—commercial or financial information, disclosure of which would cause substantial competitive injury to the submitter
5. Internal agency memorandums—protects information about an agency's decision-making process
6. Personal privacy information
7. Investigatory records—protects information compiled for law enforcement purposes, disclosure of which could reasonably interfere with enforcement proceedings or identify a confidential source
8. Special interest exemption related to banking
9. Special interest exemption regarding oil wells

Source: Freedom of Information Clearinghouse, *The Freedom of Information Act: A User's Guide* (Washington, D.C.: Freedom of Information Clearinghouse, 1989).

liberation movement, black nationalist groups, and white hate groups. A reporter with NBC News used information obtained from a FOIA request to confirm the existence of the COINTELPRO operation, which was terminated formally only after this disclosure.[50]

In 1976, the U.S. Senate's Select Committee to Study Governmental Operations with Respect to Intelligence Activities (known as the Church committee) detailed "how heavily the FBI and the CIA were involved in watching, reporting on and occasionally disrupting Americans peacefully exercising their constitutional rights."[51] Legislation was proposed, but not passed, in 1977 to curtail FBI authority to investigate domestic political groups. Many of the abuses have disappeared since Hoover's departure. Still, from 1983 to 1985, the FBI investigated the Committee in Solidarity with the People of El Salvador (CISPES), and agents interviewed American schoolchildren who wrote letters to Soviet President Mikhail Gorbachev.[52]

A number of additional tools have opened up the affairs of government to the public. These include the 1972 Federal Advisory Committee Act, which the consumer movement rallied to pass and which set uniform ground rules for the conduct of the government's 1,439 advisory committees to prevent political manipulations of technical expertise. The act, as amended in 1975, requires that meetings be open to the public, that records be kept and made available to the public, and that representation on committees be balanced and open to public scrutiny.[53]

Another information tool is the Privacy Act of 1974, which protects the public from misuse and disclosure of personal information that might be revealed under the FOIA. Under the Privacy Act, individuals have a right of access to their own files, except those from law enforcement agencies and the Central Intelligence Agency.

Using the Freedom of Information Act

The FOIA applies to every agency, department, regulatory commission, government-controlled corporation, and other body in the federal executive branch. The FOIA also applies to the Executive Office of the President and the Office of Management and Budget, but not to the president or the president's immediate staff. The act does not apply to everything that receives federal funding or to Congress, the federal courts, private corporations, or federally funded state agencies.[54]

Any individual—all U.S. citizens as well as foreign nationals—can make a request under the FOIA. Or the request can be made in the name of a corporation, partnership, or other entity, including a citizen group or press organization.[55]

Although the federal FOIA does not apply to state government agencies, all fifty states and the District of Columbia have their own laws on access to state agency information. These rules vary considerably from state to state, but most state open-government laws provide access to autopsy reports, police reports, and election records.

Much information from the federal government can be acquired through informal means. An agency's public information, press or FOIA officer may provide the information without a formal FOIA request. If an informal request fails, begin the process of applying formally for the information. A FOIA request must be in writing. Consult the sample FOIA request letter in Figure 1.

Determine exactly the information you want and which agency has it. You do not need to identify a specific document by name or title, but you must provide a description clear enough to allow a government employee familiar with an agency's files to locate the records you want.[56]

Each federal agency has an FOIA officer responsible for handling information requests. Large agencies may have FOIA officers in various subdivisions. If you know exactly which subdivision has the information, send your request to its FOIA officer. If not, the FOIA officer of the agency will forward it to the appropriate office.[57]

Figure 1

Sample Freedom of Information Act Request Letter

Your Address
Daytime Phone
Date

Freedom of Information Office
Agency
Address

Re: FOIA Request

Dear FOIA Officer:

Pursuant to the federal Freedom of Information Act, 5 U.S.C. Sec. 552, I request access to and copies of all records pertaining to (clearly describe what you want. Include identifying material, such as names, places, and the period of time about which you are inquiring. Attach news clips, reports, and other documents describing the subject of your research if you think they will help in explaining your request).

I am a college student/citizen requesting these records in a noncommercial capacity. The noncommercial capacity allows for two hours of free search time and free duplication of 100 pages. If any expenses in excess of the above would be incurred in connection with this request, please contact me before any such charges are incurred.

If my request is denied in whole or in part, I ask that you justify all deletions by reference to specific exemptions of the act. I reserve the right to appeal your decision to withhold any information.

I will expect a response within 10 business days after receipt, as the statute requires.

Thank you for your assistance.

Sincerely,

Your Name

Sources: Based on samples in Elaine P. English, *How to Use the Federal FOI Act*, 5th ed. (Washington, D.C.: FOI Service Center, 1985), pp. 20–21, and in Freedom of Information Clearinghouse, *The Freedom of Information Act: A User's Guide* (Washington, D.C.: Freedom of Information Clearinghouse, 1989).

State that the request is being made pursuant to the FOIA (5 U.S.C. Sec. 552). Write "Freedom of Information Request" on the envelope and on the letter. If possible, send the request via registered mail with return receipt requested. Keep a photocopy of your letter and your receipt.[58]

The law sets specific deadlines for replying to FOIA requests: ten working days for the initial request and twenty working days for the administrative appeal. Certain agencies chronically fail to meet the act's time requirements due to inadequate staffing and resources. The FBI often takes six to twelve months or longer to process a request fully; other agencies that have long delays include the CIA and the State and Justice departments. According to the FOI Service Center, the courts are often reluctant to enforce the FOIA's time limits as long as agencies are processing requests diligently and in good faith.[59]

Agencies may charge "reasonable" fees for the direct costs of searching for and copying the requested records, but different fees are charged according to the category or status of the requester. Students are eligible for noncommercial status, which grants them two hours of free document search time and free duplication of one hundred pages. Copies over one hundred pages generally cost 10 to 25 cents per page.[60] Ask to be notified by phone or mail if the length will exceed the free one hundred pages.

If your request is partially or entirely denied, you have the right to appeal the decision. An FOIA appeal can be filed in a simple letter. See Figure 2 for a sample appeal letter. You also have the option of filing an appeal if your request is granted but the fees are too high. If ten business days elapse after the agency receives your request and you still have not received a reply, you also have the right of appeal.[61]

Researching Elected Officials

Researching the background, voting record, and campaign finances of members of Congress, state legislators, or other elected officials lends insight to the goals, biases, obligations, and conflicts of interest that may influence the actions of officeholders. Much of the following information is specific to members of Congress but can be adapted for other elected officials.

❏ *Background Information*

Consult the resources listed here and contact the legislators' Washington or district offices for biographical information including education, family history, party affiliation, previous occupations, organization memberships, voting record on specific issues, number of terms in office, and committees and subcommittees on which the legislator serves.

The address for members of the U.S. House of Representatives is as follows:

The Honorable _____
U.S. House of Representatives
Washington, DC 20515

Figure 2

Sample Freedom of Information Act Appeal Letter

Your Address
Daytime Phone
Date

Agency Administrator
Agency
Address

Re: Freedom of Information Appeal

Dear Administrator:

This is an appeal under the Freedom of Information Act, 5 U.S.C. Sec. 552. On (date), I made an FOIA request to your agency for (brief description of what you requested). On (date), your agency denied my request on the grounds that (state the reasons given by the agency). Copies of my request and the denial are enclosed.

(Or when the agency delays) It has been ___ business days since my request was received by your agency. This period clearly exceeds the 10 days provided by the statute; hence I deem my request denied. Copies of my correspondence and the postal form showing receipt by your office are enclosed.

The information that I have requested is clearly releasable under the FOIA and, in my opinion, may not be protected validly by any of the act's exemptions.

(Here, address why you think the agency's justification for a specific exemption is incorrect.)

I trust that upon reconsideration, you will reverse the decision denying me access to this material and grant my original request.

As I have made this request in a noncommercial capacity and this information is of timely value, I would appreciate your expediting the consideration of my appeal in every way possible. In any case, I will expect to receive your decision within 20 business days, as required by the statute.

Thank you for your assistance.

Sincerely,

Your Name

Sources: Based on samples in Elaine P. English, *How to Use the Federal FOI Act*, 5th ed. (Washington, D.C.: FOI Service Center, 1985), pp. 20–21, and in Freedom of Information Clearinghouse, *The Freedom of Information Act: A User's Guide* (Washington, D.C.: Freedom of Information Clearinghouse, 1989).

Address for U.S. Senators is as follows:

The Honorable _____
U.S. Senate
Washington, DC 20510

Some of these directories may be in your public or university library:

Congressional Directory. Published annually by the Superintendent of Documents, U.S. Government Printing Office, Washington, DC 20402; $15. Contains biographical information on members of Congress, lists committee assignments and staff, and names federal agency officials.

Who's Who in Congress. Published annually by Congressional Quarterly, 1414 22nd Street, N.W., Washington, DC 20037; $7.95. A pocket-size guide to Congress including biographical data, phone numbers, staff, committee assignments, election results, CQ's vote studies (frequency of voting and percentage of votes aligned with legislator's party and with the president), rankings from four interest groups, and votes on selected key votes (with an explanation of why).

Politics in America. Published annually by Congressional Quarterly, 1414 22nd Street, N.W., Washington, DC 20037; $39.95. Detailed profiles of all members of Congress, election results, campaign finance data, interest group ratings, CQ's voting studies.

Congressional Yellow Book. Published quarterly by the Monitor Publishing Company, 104 Fifth Avenue, New York, NY 10011; $175 yearly subscription includes four editions. Brief biographical information on each member of Congress, staff, committee and subcommittee assignments, leadership positions, and membership in official groups and informal caucuses.

State Yellow Book. Published twice a year by the Monitor Publishing Company, 104 Fifth Avenue, New York, NY 10011; $150 yearly subscription includes two volumes. Directory of executive and legislative branches of all fifty states, the District of Columbia, and the four insular U.S. territories including demographics, history, state maps, and geographical information; economic and education data; and sources for obtaining public records.

Congressional Staff Directory. Published twice a year by Staff Directories, Ltd., P.O. Box 62, Mount Vernon, VA 22121; $59. Includes biographies of all members of Congress as well as their key staff and committees and subcommittees.

Almanac of American Politics. Published every two years by the National Journal, 1730 M Street, N.W., Washington, DC 20036; $44.95. Contains biographical information on members of Congress and state governors and statistical information on their records, states, and districts.

❏ *Congressional Districts*

Data about congressional districts' population; minority representation; breakdown by urban, rural, and metropolitan areas; median age; median income; education; occupations; and economy can be found in the following sources.

Congressional District Atlas. Published every two years by the U.S. Government Printing Office, Washington, DC 20402; $33. Contains maps of districts, counties, and municipalities, and statistical information about these areas.

Congressional Districts Wall Map. Published periodically by the Superintendent of Documents, U.S. Bureau of the Census, DPD, Public Unit, 1201 East 10th Street, Jeffersonville, IN 47132. The 1987 map is available for $4.75.

Congress Poster. Published by Congressional Quarterly, 1414 22nd Street, N.W., Washington, DC 20037; $14.95. The map shows congressional districts, including every senator and representative and party affiliation as of the November 1990 elections.

Congressional Districts in the 1990s. Published by Congressional Quarterly, 1414 22nd Street, N.W., Washington, DC 20037. Contains complete demographic and political profiles of all 435 congressional districts. Updated after census data become available at the turn of each decade.

❏ *Sponsorship of Legislation and Voting Record*

Legislation introduced by legislators is often dictated by the committees on which they sit. But legislators can sign on as cosponsors of any bill under consideration. Sponsorship indicates the types of issues a legislator considers important.

How an elected official votes is the primary indicator of performance in the office. Consumer, environmental, labor, and other citizen groups compile voting score cards to identify members of Congress with favorable or unfavorable voting records on legislation of interest to their group. Environmental Action has developed a "Dirty Dozen" list of the members of Congress who had, in their view, the worst voting records on environmental issues. Environmental Action distributes the list nationwide to members, other interest groups, and the media. *Congressional Quarterly* tabulates the frequency with which legislators vote and how often they vote with their party for a variety of issues.

Congressional documents such as bills, committee reports, presidential messages to Congress, resolutions, and public laws may be obtained free by writing the offices listed. Include the bill number or a clear document reference and a self-addressed label.

House Document Room, U.S. House of Representatives, 2nd and D Streets, SW, B-18, Washington, DC 20515.

Senate Document Room, U.S. Senate, Hart Building, Washington, DC 20510.

Committee documents such as legislative calendars of committee activity listing every bill referred to the committee and what action has been taken; listings of all recent committee documents, including hearings (with transcripts of witness testimony) and committee reports on legislation and special studies; and committee rules may be obtained free of charge by writing to your congressional representative or to the relevant committee (at the address listed above for members of Congress).

Congressional Record. Published each day Congress is in session by the Superintendent of Documents, U.S. Government Printing Office, Washington, DC 20402; yearly subscription, $225 (paper), $118 (microfiche); $1.50 per issue. Contains all legislative activity for that particular day, floor debate and votes, bills introduced, committee reports filed, schedules of committee hearings, and speeches.

LEGIS. This legislative information service by phone will provide a list of all legislation sponsored by any member of Congress during the current or past session of Congress. It will send a printout of the information at no cost. Clerk of the House, Office of Legislative Information, House Office Building Annex 2, 3rd and D Streets, S.W., Room 696, Washington, DC 20515; (202) 225-1772.

Congressional Quarterly Almanac. Published annually by Congressional Quarterly, 1414 22nd Street, N.W., Washington, DC 20027; $195. Contains a summary, organized by topic, of all legislative activity for the previous session. A particularly good source for interpreting legislation.

Congressional Quarterly Weekly Report. Published weekly when Congress is in session by Congressional Quarterly, 1414 22nd Street, N.W., Washington, DC 20037. Provides information on congressional activities, progress on major bills, voting and activities of legislators, news events affecting Congress, and background on issues.

Congressional Roll Call. Published at the end of each session of Congress by Congressional Quarterly, 1414 22nd Street, N.W., Washington, DC 20037; $19.95. Includes a chronology and analysis of all House and Senate roll-call votes.

Congressional Index. Published monthly, with quarterly and annual cumulative volumes, by the Congressional Index Service, 4520 East-West Highway, Suite 800, Bethesda, MD 20814. Indexes congressional publications since 1970 and includes summaries of hearings, reports, and other congressional documents and provides an index by subject, author, witness, and so on.

The following groups rate the members of Congress according to their voting records on specific issues of interest to them and develop score cards or voting record reports with that information. Most copies are free.

American Conservative Union (conservative issues; $2.00)
38 Ivy Street, S.E.
Washington, DC 20003

American Federation of Labor and Congress of Industrial
Organizations (AFL-CIO) (economic and labor issues)
815 16th Street, N.W.
Washington, DC 20006

Americans for Democratic Action (liberal issues; $5.00)
1511 K Street, N.W., Suite 941
Washington, DC 20005

Children's Defense Fund (children's issues)
122 C Street, N.W.
Washington, DC 20006

Common Cause (good-government issues)
2030 M Street, N.W.
Washington, DC 20036

Congressional Quarterly (major issues)
1414 22nd Street, N.W.
Washington, DC 20037

Consumer Federation of America (consumer issues; $10.00)
1424 16th Street, N.W.
Washington, DC 20036

Environmental Action (environmental issues)
6930 Carrol Avenue, Suite 600
Takoma Park, MD 20912

Friends Committee on National Legislation (peace issues)
245 2nd Street, N.E.
Washington, DC 20002

Leadership Conference on Civil Rights (civil rights issues)
2027 Massachusetts Avenue, N.W.
Washington, DC 20036

League of Conservation Voters (environmental issues; $3.00)
1150 Connecticut Avenue, N.W.
Washington, DC 20036

National Association for the Advancement of Colored People
(African American issues)
1025 Vermont Avenue, N.W.
Washington, DC 20036

National Council of Senior Citizens (seniors' issues)
1511 K Street, N.W.
Washington, DC 20005

National Education Association (education and teachers' issues)
1201 16th Street, N.W.
Washington, DC 20036

National Farmers Union (agricultural issues)
600 Maryland Avenue, S.E.
Washington, DC 20024

National Women's Political Caucus (women's issues)
1275 K Street, N.W., Suite 750
Washington, DC 20005

Public Citizen's Congress Watch (consumer issues; $5.00)
215 Pennsylvania Avenue, S.E.
Washington, DC 20003

U.S. Chamber of Commerce (business and industry issues)
1615 H Street, N.W.
Washington, DC 20062

❏ *Innovative Work and Views on Important Issues*

Some legislators are unusually persistent or creative in attracting attention to problems or issues they consider particularly important and in trying to pass legislation to address those problems. For example, former Wisconsin Senator William Proxmire gave his monthly Golden Fleece Award to "the biggest example of ridiculous, ironic or wasteful government spending."[62]

❏ *Media Coverage*

Coverage of legislators by local newspapers, television, and radio is a source of general information. Check national newsmagazines, including *Time, Newsweek,* and *U.S. News and World Report,* and national papers like the *Wall Street Journal,* the *Washington Post,* the *New York Times,* or the *Los Angeles Times* as well as coverage in smaller circulation publications such as newsletters and journals.

❏ *Campaign Finance*

Looking at sources of campaign contributions can reveal a great deal about a legislator's affiliations, allegiances, and obligations. As journalist Penny Loeb writes, "It's not enough just to list who gives what to which candidate or what investments a candidate has. The real story is why a person or business gives something to a candidate—and what they get in return."[63]

The cost of running a campaign for public office—especially for Congress—is growing rapidly. The average cost in 1990 of winning a seat in the U.S. Senate was nearly $4 million, more than six times what it cost in 1976.[64] The increase is due largely to increases in the cost of television and radio advertising and postage rates. The amount of money needed is so high that members of Congress must spend a large amount of their time in office raising money for the next election. For example, a member of the House has to raise an average of $17,000 a month during a two-year term, and senators must raise almost $56,000 a month during a six-year term.[65]

Campaign funding sources, when compared to the legislators' voting records and committee assignments, can identify potential conflicts of interest. Be careful not to jump to conclusions, but do raise questions about the potential for a conflict.

Candidates for Congress (and president) are required to report all contributions of $200 or more from individuals, all contributions of any size from political action committees and political party committees, and all bank loans.[66] PACs and political parties are also required to report when and where they spend money. Thus you can research all the contributions to a particular candidate's campaign or all the candidates to whom a PAC or party gave funds.

The Federal Elections Commission (FEC) keeps records for all federal campaigns. Microfilm cartridges, which are the official FEC record, contain information dating back to the 1972 elections. Computer indexes provide detailed campaign finance information beginning with the 1977–1978 election cycle. Most computer record printouts are free to students.

A detailed pamphlet, *Using FEC Campaign Finance Information*, listing available FEC records, can be obtained free of charge. Write or call the Federal Election Commission, Public Records Office, 999 E Street, N.W., Washington, DC 20463; (800) 424-9530.

The FEC provides various educational services free of charge, including audiovisual materials, publications, and speakers. Publications include *Supporting Federal Candidates: A Guide for Citizens* and *The Federal Election Commission: The First 10 Years, 1975–1985.*

Laws on campaign finance disclosure for state and local elections vary from state to state. Contact the state board of elections for specific information.

Common Cause and Public Citizen's Congress Watch both publish studies and reports on PAC contributions, personal financial holdings, honoraria, and proposals for campaign finance reform.

❑ *Personal Finances*

Personal finances, like campaign funds, have the potential to create conflicts of interest. Reviewing personal financial information; making note of any connections with corporations, banks, or interest groups; and comparing these connections with committees on which the legislator sits, legislation introduced, and voting records may identify potential areas of conflict of interest.

The Ethics in Government Act of 1978 requires limited disclosure of information concerning personal finances. Members of the House of Representatives must list all business and professional income of more than $100 or stocks worth over $1,000. Senators must disclose all speaking fees and all income from honoraria, dividends, interest, rent, capital gains, trusts, estates, and other sources; gifts of transportation, lodging, food, or entertainment; reimbursements; property; liabilities and other financial information; nongovernment positions held; agreements for future employment or continuation of payments or benefits; and blind-trust financial arrangements. What must be reported is subject to various minimum or maximum amounts.

The reports filed by each representative and each senator are due on May 15 of each year and are released to the public on June 14. Reports for the House of Representatives are available at the Office of Records and Registration, 1036 Longworth House Office Building, Washington, DC 20515. Senate reports are available at the Office of Public Records, 232 Hart Senate Office Building, Washington, DC 20510. Individual copies of Senate reports, but not House reports, are available through the mail from the above address for a copying charge of 20 cents a page.

The reports are also on file at the office of each state's secretary of state for all members of that state's congressional delegation and for each of the state's two U.S. senators. Reports for the House of Representatives, but not the Senate, are available at all federal depository libraries.

Members of Congress also are required to report expenditures, including mass mailings; foreign gifts received; foreign travel; and conflict-of-interest statements for outside business or employment activity. This information is available in the following two reports:

Report of the Secretary of the Senate. Published twice a year by the Secretary of the Senate, 5208 U.S. Capitol Building, Washington, DC 20510; free.

Report of the Clerk of the House. Published twice a year by the Clerk of the House, H-105 U.S. Capitol Building, Washington, DC 20515; free.

In addition, Public Citizen's Congress Watch publishes a report on publicly and privately funded travel expenditures by members of Congress.

DIRECT ACTION

Direct actions "happen when a group of people takes collective action to confront a designated target with a set of specific demands. The group action involves people *directly* with the issue, using their numbers as a means of pressuring an opponent."[67]

Boycott

A boycott is "an organized consumer refusal to buy a product or to buy from a particular seller."[68] The purpose of a boycott is to put economic pressure on a business to change a policy. Boycotts range from individual to international efforts to protest unfair or unethical practices of a company or an organization.

"Because the average retail outlet depends on so many customers, it's often very difficult for people's organizations to really cut off very much of their trade," explains Si Kahn.[69] In addition, effective boycotts require significant amounts of time, energy, and money. Most groups try to negotiate with the targeted business before launching a boycott. The legality of boycotts is also a factor to consider. Although the U.S. Supreme Court in 1988 significantly expanded the right of unions to use secondary boycotts—those that affect the business of a company not involved in the main dispute—in general, legal boycotts must be directed at the business directly involved in the dispute.[70]

Despite the numerous obstacles, boycotts are often effective in pressuring a business to change its policies. Even if sales are affected only slightly, boycotts generate negative publicity, and the image of the business suffers. Boycotts were a popular tactic of the American colonists, who refused to buy numerous British goods to protest English policies the colonists thought unfair. In 1991, according to the Seattle-based Institute for Consumer Responsibility, groups throughout the United States were carrying out over three hundred nationwide boycotts.[71]

An international boycott of the Swiss corporation Nestlé, the world's largest seller of infant formula, organized by the Infant Formula Action Coalition (INFACT), began in 1977 to protest Nestlé's aggressive promotion of its infant formula product to new mothers in developing countries. According to Nancy Gaschott of Action for Corporate Accountability (ACTION), "Mothers—particularly in the developing countries—who don't have clean water and high incomes are not able to prepare feeding bottles safely. Mixed with bacteria-laden water and over-diluted to make it last longer, the expensive artificial milk becomes a daily dose of disease and malnutrition." The United Nations estimates that 1 million infants die annually because they are bottle-fed rather than breast-fed.[72]

Used properly, with clean water and at the recommended doses, infant formula is a safe substitute for mother's milk for the small number of women who cannot breast-feed. Yet for the majority of mothers, breast-feeding is not only cheaper but also more beneficial for infants because breast milk provides both adequate nutrition and immunizing agents to protect against disease.[73]

To encourage the use of infant formula, its manufacturers provided hospitals with free samples to give to mothers of newborns.[74] The mothers become dependent on the infant formula when their milk dries up and must continue to buy formula when the samples run out. In addition, infant formula manufacturers also hire "milk nurses" to visit mothers in maternity wards to promote bottle-feeding as better for the baby than breast-feeding.[75]

Citizen groups, concerned health workers, and churches began in the early 1970s to pressure infant formula manufacturers to stop their aggressive promotion of bottle-feeding. Ten years later, various manufacturers did stop the most blatant forms of marketing but continued to distribute free samples.[76] Citizen groups responded with the Nestlé boycott, which "developed into one of the largest battles ever waged against corporate power by citizen groups, with over 100 organizations in some 65 countries joining in."[77]

Citizen groups also turned to the United Nations World Health Organization (WHO), which in 1981 passed the International Code of Marketing of Breastmilk Substitutes, which prohibits certain sales tactics, including free hospital samples used as a sales inducement, and urged hospital health professionals to support breast-feeding. The United States was the only country in the United Nations to vote against the code.[78]

In 1984, INFACT ended the Nestlé boycott when Nestlé agreed to abide by the WHO code. However, critics of Nestlé continued to monitor the company's sales practices to ensure that compliance measures were carried out.[79] In October 1988, ACTION announced a new boycott against Nestlé and the American Home Products (AHP) corporation. ACTION discovered that Nestlé and AHP had violated the WHO code by providing hospitals with free samples of infant formula. Shortly after the new boycott was launched, organizations in twenty countries lent their support.[80]

Picketing

Picketing, often combined with other forms of direct action such as boycotts and strikes, can be an effective way to publicize complaints and pressure a target to change its policies.

The first reported consumer picket, in New York City in 1934, involved a neighborhood group protesting a local bakery that had raised the cost of its bread. In the resulting court case, *Julie Baking Co., Inc., v. Graymond*, the court upheld the right to picket, with restrictions on the number of people and hours during which the group could protest.[81]

Various laws regulating picketing stipulate that at least one picketer must have a genuine dispute with the target of the picket; the picketers may not ask the business to do anything unlawful or call for the closing of the business; they must not make false claims or exaggerations, may not use violence or abusive language or create a disturbance, and may not prevent people from walking on the sidewalk or entering and leaving the business; and the place of the picketing should be related to its purpose.[82] In addition, states or towns may require that demonstrators obtain a permit before picketing. The courts often overturn local ordinances restricting picketing.

Demonstrations and Protests

Protests, public demonstrations, and marches can be effective on a mass scale or with only a small group of people. Such protests increase public awareness and show public support for an issue. In one of the largest political demonstrations in U.S. history, 750,000 people gathered in New York City's Central Park in June 1982 to support the citizen campaign for a freeze on nuclear weapons production.[83] In April 1993, 600,000 advocates of civil rights for lesbian and gay people participated in a march and rally in Washington, D.C., organized by the Human Rights Campaign Fund and the National Gay and Lesbian Task Force.

Protests or marches usually require a permit. The laws vary in different cities; the police department is a good place to begin a search for local requirements.

Strikes

In a strike, employees refuse to work, interrupting the normal flow of business at a workplace. Strikes, most commonly used as a bargaining weapon by labor unions, can persuade an employer to listen to employees because the company cannot produce without the workers.[84]

Until passage of the National Labor Relations Act of 1935, the right of workers to unionize was not recognized under federal law. Workers used the strike to force employers to recognize the union as their bargaining representative. Although the Taft-Hartley Act of 1947 placed significant restrictions on workers' right to strike, unions continue to use strikes to win wage increases, health and pension plans, and improved working conditions.

In 1985, the U.S. Supreme Court upheld the right—established in a 1938 decision—of employers "to use permanent replacement workers in instances where their workforce strikes for economic reasons." By hiring permanent replacement workers, or threatening to do so, employers "undercut labor's bargaining power by drastically curtailing its ability to make use of its most potent weapon, the strike."[85] The number of strikes called by labor decreased dramatically during the 1980s—from 187 in 1980 to only 54 in 1985 and 44 in 1990.[86] Labor unions continue to work to convince Congress to pass legislation that would prohibit employers from hiring permanent replacements for striking workers.[87]

Authorized strikes are those agreed to in advance by union officials or a majority of the union members. Wildcat strikes are called by a group of workers without official union support. Most strikes are walkouts, when workers leave their jobs. In a sit-down strike, workers stop working but do not leave their place of employment. A sympathy strike is called by one union to support another union that is on strike. A jurisdictional strike results when two or more rival unions claim the right to work on the same job. A secondary strike occurs when workers call a work stoppage to try to force their employer to stop doing business with another employer who is involved in a labor dispute.

When a strike begins, union members usually set up picket lines at the business's entrances. The purpose of the picket line is to explain the reason for the strike, to turn away replacement workers, to discourage customers, and to keep goods from being taken into or out of the building. Union members usually refuse to cross the picket line of another union.

Nonviolent Civil Disobedience

Civil disobedience is the act of refusing to obey a specific law to protest the law or government policies or priorities. African Americans used nonviolent civil disobedience extensively during the civil rights movement to protest laws that segregated public facilities and that made it difficult or impossible to register and vote. Rosa Parks, secretary of the Alabama chapter of the National Association for the Advancement of Colored People, broke the law when she refused to give up her seat on a Montgomery, Alabama, bus to a white man. Parks's act of civil disobedience triggered a bus boycott that succeeded in desegregating public buses in Montgomery.[88]

The sit-in is a form of nonviolent civil disobedience that students, beginning with a lunch counter sit-in in Greensboro, North Carolina, in 1960, used to force more than one hundred southern communities to end segregation in public places.[89]

Another type of civil disobedience is tax resistance—refusing to pay all or part of income tax owed to protest government policies, usually those relating to issues of war and peace. Many tax resisters file their income tax forms with the Internal Revenue Service (IRS) every year, and many enclose letters of protest instead of a check. The IRS may respond by seizing bank accounts, paychecks, and property, to collect the tax owed and interest. But many of the thousands of resisters who withhold payment do so as a matter of conscience, not because of a proven effectiveness in changing policy.[90]

CITIZEN LOBBYING

Lobbying is the act of persuading legislators or other policy makers to change an existing law or policy, create a new one, or reject a change under consideration. The methods are basically the same whether trying to influence university administrators, city or county officials, state legislators, or members of Congress.

Decision makers are influenced by numerous factors including party affiliation, interests of campaign contributors, personal views and experience, and public opinion. The job of the lobbyist is to find out which decision makers have not made up their minds or which can be persuaded to change them. Of course, other lobbyists will try to persuade the same legislators to vote the other way.

One of the most effective persuasion tactics citizen groups have is to show public support for a policy. Members of Congress, state legislators, or city council members who want to be reelected listen to their constituents. By showing that large numbers of constituents favor your bill or proposal, you can influence votes.

Public support, however, is rarely enough to pass legislation. An understanding of the legislative or decision-making process, as well as knowing who the key players are, is essential to effective lobbying in Congress, state legislatures, county boards, and city halls.

This section concentrates on the legislative process followed by Congress and most state legislatures, but much of the advice can be applied to city or county councils.

Identifying the Key Players

In a legislative campaign, start by identifying the most powerful legislators, including the chairs of committees and party leaders. Marc Caplan, in *A Citizens' Guide to Lobbying*, suggests that citizen lobbyists "check records of past legislative sessions, which may include transcripts of public hearings and floor debates, lists of bills and their sponsors, and records of votes. . . . Read these to learn the key players and the lines of debate on each bill."[91] For more on identifying legislators' motivations, see the section on researching elected officials.

Because it is nearly impossible for a bill (a proposed law) to reach the full legislative body without first being considered in a committee, the committee with jurisdiction over your issue plays an important role. Identify committee members, particularly the chairperson. Determine how each committee member has voted on similar issues. Committee staffers are important contacts because they often specialize in particular issue areas, manage much of the information legislators receive, and set priorities for issues, and they can be instrumental in scheduling and providing access to important information.[92]

Become familiar with the various publications of the relevant governmental body to keep track of action in the current session. For instance, most legislatures publish a daily calendar of bills up for action in each house; a bulletin listing committee meetings, public hearings, and other events; and a journal recording activity from the day before.[93]

Writing a Bill and Finding a Sponsor

Ask legislators what laws dealing with the issue you want to solve exist or are under consideration. Ask which members of which committees and which agencies handle such laws. Read copies of relevant laws, bills, resolutions, and committee reports.[94]

If you determine that no bill exists to deal with your issue of concern, you can write your own. Writing a bill precisely is important. As Marc Caplan explains, "Shoddy draftsmanship gives opponents and potential supporters an easy excuse to oppose a bill, and gives you a reputation for carelessness." A lawyer is a valuable ally in writing legislation.[95]

Thorough research is essential. Whatever your proposal, be it a new federal law or a change in school policy, determine the immediate and future costs, how the funds will be provided, who benefits, and why federal (or state or local) action is necessary.[96] The American Bar Association, the Council of State Governments, and the American Law Institute publish collections of model legislation on various issues each year that may help you get started.[97] Contact other citizen groups that have succeeded in passing similar measures. For example, citizen groups have worked in many states to pass laws, which can be duplicated in your state, to require deposits on bottles and cans. Citing successes from another state, city, or school also gives the measure credibility.[98]

In the legislature, once the bill is written, a member of Congress or state legislator must sponsor and introduce it. Your representative may not be the best person to introduce your bill. Rather, it is important to have someone who sits on the relevant committee introduce it. In addition, Mark Green and colleagues advise, "beware of the token bill," introduced by legislators to fulfill their responsibilities to constituents and then left to die without further attention from the legislator.[99]

You need a sponsor who is committed and will work hard. The chairperson of the committee that will consider the bill is your best bet, but legislators who have sponsored similar bills or advocated similar issues are also good choices.[100]

Introducing a bill in both houses of the legislature at the same time greatly speeds up the process because both houses must pass exactly the same bill. If the two houses end up with different versions, the bill must go to a conference committee, composed of members from each house to work out a compromise.

Committee Hearings

Every bill is referred to an appropriate committee or subcommittee. Writes Marc Caplan, "This is the first hurdle for a bill. It is relatively simple for legislative leaders to kill a bill by referring it to a committee opposed to it."[101]

The committees hold hearings on most bills to gather information from different points of view. Mark Green and colleagues advise that "testimony is an important way to educate committee members, committee staff and the press. To ensure that your position gets a fair airing, you should help recruit relevant witnesses. . . . You needn't be a professional 'expert' in order to testify effectively. Often personal experience and passion count far more than learning or polish."[102]

Testimony in these hearings needs to be in plain English, preferably spoken, not read. Prepare to answer questions from opponents. Gimmicks or dramatic testimony from people affected personally by the issue often are successful in stressing a point and capture the attention of the public and the media. "During hearings on the coal mine health and safety bill, miners with severe black lung gripped the attention of [committee members] by showing how they collapsed from lack of breath after jumping up and down just a few times," write Mark Green and colleagues.[103] Testimony is recorded in the official transcript of the hearing, so prepare written copies for the record and for distribution to members of the committee and members of the press.[104]

Hearings are held at all levels of government and in some university administrations. Find out the procedure for participating in city or county council or university hearings. If no such process exists, work to implement a mechanism that allows students to voice their concerns.

In the legislative process, the committee staff typically prepare a draft committee bill after the hearings. The committee meets in a mark-up session to go over the draft and propose amendments. Mark-up sessions are where many details of bills are decided. At this point the committee may vote on the bill, refer it to another committee, amend it to weaken its effect, or ignore it. If the vote is favorable, it goes before the full house of the legislature in which it was introduced.

Once the bill reaches the floor, lobbyists attempt to persuade all legislators of the importance of the measure. Call legislators' offices to determine how they plan to vote, categorizing each as yes, no, or undecided. Personally contact those who need persuading, and call on the public to apply pressure as well. Ask sponsors and supporters to speak on the floor in support of the bill.[105]

Persuasion Tactics

In attempting to win votes, citizen groups use a variety of tactics to inform legislators, other decision makers, and the public of the importance of proposed legislation. Legislators are most responsive when they know their constituents are following their actions on a particular issue. A citizen or student lobby must show that the public or the student body cares about and supports the proposed legislation or other policy change. Some common tactics include petitions, letter-writing campaigns, telegrams, telephone calls, personal visits with legislators, and forming coalitions with other organizations.

"Legislators hear nothing from their constituents on the vast majority of bills. When they do get a few letters or telephone calls, they take notice. Sometimes a handful of calls can change a vote. On a controversial issue, much more is needed," writes Marc Caplan.[106]

Legislators rarely read all the letters that come into their offices, but most have their staff take a count to see where people stand. The most effective letter-writing campaigns are those with large numbers of individually written letters rather than form letters. Telegrams and telephone calls are particularly effective just before a vote: they let legislators know that constituents are watching their vote.[107]

Petitions—short written statements of support—are most impressive when enough people have signed to show that more than a few people care about the issue and that the signatures represent an organized constituency. Signatures on petitions represent possible votes to decision makers. Common ways to gather signatures for petitions include canvassing door to door and setting up tables at shopping malls, supermarkets, or schools or in other heavily traveled areas.

Visiting a legislator, city official, or school administrator gives citizen or student groups an opportunity to explain face to face the importance of their bill or proposal and to demonstrate the depth of support. Mark Green and colleagues advise that "in personal lobbying it is also essential *to get exact commitments*." A legislator may fulfill a promise to vote "pro-education" only by voting yes on a weak bill after undermining stronger versions in the committee.[108]

Citizen lobbies form coalitions to increase their effectiveness. Coalitions often send letters to let decision makers know that groups have banded together in support of or opposition to a bill or policy.

After a Bill Is Passed

The process is not over when a bill is passed. Except in North Carolina, where the governor has no veto power, the executive may veto or refuse to spend all the money appropriated by the legislature.[109] And the agency responsible for carrying out the program may write ineffective regulations or simply may not enforce the law's provisions.[110] Citizen and student groups must monitor implementation of laws and policies and continue to pressure decision makers to ensure enforcement.

Student Lobbyist in Action: Jill Siegel

State University of New York at Buffalo student Jill Siegel, at age nineteen, successfully lobbied the New York state legislature to pass a bill designed to protect consumers from fraud in sales of hearing aids, despite intense opposition from the hearing aid industry. Siegel's campaign was part of her legislative internship with the student group New York Public Interest Research Group (NYPIRG). "From being a nervous and up-tight sophomore, I became more aggressive and poised as I went along," Siegel explains.[111]

NYPIRG students at Queens College had released a study revealing that hearing aid dealers regularly convinced elderly customers to buy the devices whether or not they needed them and that dealers failed to alert customers who needed further medical attention. Siegel and the NYPIRG staff proposed that a law be passed to require all hearing aid customers to obtain a doctor's prescription before purchase to ensure that only those who need the device buy it. "Once when our bill got stalled, we held a press conference with the sponsors," Siegel recalls. "We put together a good campaign—lots of letters and telegrams—from hundreds of people. On such a relatively obscure issue, that much support is unexpected. It makes people pay a lot of attention."[112]

NYPIRG formed a coalition with senior citizen groups, doctors, and audiologists that effectively pressured the legislature to pass the bill. Siegel says, "Being there first hand was what really taught me about the legislature. . . . I always have felt that through college most of my true learning was gleaned from working with NYPIRG."[113]

THE COURTS

Lawsuits

Citizen groups, particularly in the civil rights and environmental move-ments, have won major victories through the courts. The courts are an important mechanism to force the government to implement or enforce existing laws, to seek compensation for injury or harm, and to obtain restraining orders.

Citizen groups frequently use litigation to force government agencies to take action when the agency is not enforcing a law, not acting within a prescribed time limit, or in some other way not fulfilling its legal obliga-tions. Because many federal agencies rarely have the funding required to enforce all the laws and regulations on the books properly, a lawsuit can help set priorities for government agencies by requiring them to choose one enforcement action over another.[114] Although many judges hesitate to change an agency's decision, if the decision appears to be arbitrary or based on inadequate or inappropriate information, the court often will force the agency to adopt a different course of action.[115]

A number of federal environmental laws contain specific provisions that allow citizens to sue when the law is not being enforced. For instance, citizen suit provisions allow for instance, any citizen to sue in federal court a polluter who is violating federal law or the terms of its permit. Citizens can sue the Environmental Protection Agency administrator for failing to enforce the law.[116]

A court will allow a suit only after the agency has taken final action and after administrative remedies are exhausted.[117] Many agencies have a hearing process to give the public an opportunity to voice disagreement with a decision or proposal. The hearing process is especially important in environmental issues where federal law requires companies to apply for permits before discharging pollutants.[118]

A class action suit is one in which a plaintiff (the person bringing the suit) represents a number of people charging similar damage. Such a suit is one way to win financial compensation for an injury or some other action from the offender. Often individuals cannot afford the cost and time to sue by themselves; class actions allows plaintiffs to pool their resources. In class action suits, the courts generally require that all poten-tial plaintiffs be notified.

Injunctions and Orders

Courts can issue emergency relief orders when a situation presents an immediate danger. Temporary restraining orders or preliminary injunc-tions are sought when clear and irreparable damage would occur without immediate court intervention. The orders are issued for a period of a few days or until a hearing or trial can be scheduled.

Many factors apply in filing a suit. To sue, the injured person, the plaintiff, must have "standing," that is, must have a sufficient interest in or be directly affected by the problem in question. Cases must also be filed within the statute of limitations, the period of time during which a defendant, the person being sued, remains responsible for a problem. The statute of limitations is particularly troublesome in cases where health problems related to chemical exposure, for example, appear a great many year after the exposure.

Lawyers are usually necessary to carry out the technical aspects of the case. To find a lawyer familiar with your type of case, talk with other organizations that have brought similar suits. Public interest and advocacy groups may have lawyers interested in your case, and some law schools have legal clinics to provide advice and handle cases at no charge.

Bringing a case to court is a long and often expensive process. A lawsuit can take several years, depending on the complexity of the case. In most lawsuits in which financial compensation for injured parties is sought, plaintiffs pay the lawyer nothing unless they receive money from the defendant. This form of payment is called a contingency fee. In a successful suit, the plaintiff pays the lawyer anywhere from 20 to 40 percent of the amount won.[119] In addition to attorneys' fees, plaintiffs may be required to pay filing fees, photocopying costs, telephone bills, and travel and fees for witnesses. Some law firms that ordinarily charge high fees also take a few cases each year on a pro bono basis, or for the public good.[120]

In addition, free legal help for people who cannot afford to hire a lawyer due to a low income may be available through legal aid and legal services, depending on the issue. The offices are often so understaffed that they cannot handle all the cases that come to them.[121]

Small Claims Court

Small claims courts, which differ from state to state, are primarily informal courts with simplified procedures set up to enable people to collect small amounts of money without hiring a lawyer in cases such as disputes between landlords and tenants. The majority of plaintiffs win but often do not receive all the money they request.[122]

People can take a case to small claims court after trying to resolve the problem in other ways, when they know who is responsible, and when a dollar value, actual or estimated, can be put on their loss. The most frequent small claims court cases are those "compelling people to pay money agreed to in a contract and getting compensation for services performed."[123]

To locate a small claims court, call the clerk or information office of any of the lower noncriminal courts. Many courts, as well as consumer agencies or groups, publish materials that describe how the court works. Before going to court to file a claim, the plaintiff must find the precise legal name of the person or business involved in the dispute. Most businesses and landlords must register with the government or file for a license to operate a business. Check with the county clerk, secretary of state, licensing boards, and tax offices.[124]

Plaintiffs can sue for all expenses, up to the court's limit, including transportation costs, phone bills, and wages lost. The court can decrease (but not increase) the amount requested. The court will notify the defendant, who must appear in court or give up the right to have the case heard. Make sure all witnesses are present, and, if necessary, get a subpoena ordering them to appear. Prepare all records, such as canceled checks or receipts, and attach a brief summary to any that are long or complex. Remember that at any time before the case, both parties can reach a compromise or settlement. If this happens, the settlement must be in writing and signed by both parties.[125]

Be on time for the trial, and have all the necessary papers. The average small claims case takes twenty minutes, so be concise. Small claims court judges often help people present their cases and may ask witnesses questions. The court's decision will be given at the end of the trial or by mail within a few weeks.[126]

Winning plaintiffs often have trouble collecting on decisions in small claims court. Collection procedures vary, but they generally require that the plaintiff make sure that the judgment has been formally registered in the court's books. Then a sheriff or marshal may be asked to obtain a court order to seize a defendant's assets or wages to collect what is owed.[127]

INITIATIVE AND REFERENDUM

The initiative and referendum process is the closest thing the United States has to direct democracy. Citizens enact or reject laws directly at the voting booth rather than through elected officials. An initiative is a new law proposed by citizens placed on the ballot by a petition bearing the signatures of a specified number of voters. In a referendum, a law already approved by elected officials is placed on the ballot either by citizen petition or by the officials.

Initiative and referendum were popular techniques during the Populist farmers' movement and the Progressive reform era. The state of Oregon adopted the initiative and referendum process in 1904—second only to South Dakota in 1898—and in the next ten years passed initiatives to implement direct election of U.S. senators, establish the nation's first presidential primary, eliminate the poll tax, and extend the right to vote to women. By the end of World War I, twenty states had adopted the initiative and referendum process.[128]

The techniques regained popularity in the 1970s, and since then citizen groups have used them to work on tax reform, environmental problems, and voter registration reforms and to oppose nuclear power. In 1977, a group of citizens campaigned to amend the U.S. Constitution to allow voters to pass laws nationally using the initiative, but the proposal died in both Senate and House committees. Neither does the United States have a national referendum process. Consequently, initiative and referendum issues must fall under state or local jurisdictions.

Citizen groups turn to initiatives when state legislators or city officials refuse to respond to an issue, despite public opinion. Even defeated initiatives, as well as those that never reach the ballot, have spurred state legislatures to take action on issues that concern the public.

The following state constitutions allow for voter initiatives: Alaska, Arizona, Arkansas, California, Colorado, Florida, Idaho, Illinois, Maine, Michigan, Missouri, Massachusetts, Montana, Nebraska, Nevada, North Dakota, Ohio, Oklahoma, Oregon, South Dakota, Utah, Washington, and Wyoming. Of these, only Florida and Illinois do not have referendum provisions. New Mexico and Maryland have statewide provisions for referendums but not initiatives.[129]

When one or more individuals decide that a new law is needed but elected officials are unlikely to pass it, they may consider an initiative campaign. Citizens should first consult with their representative at the state or local level about bills dealing with the issue. If no bills are currently under consideration, a group of citizens may ask that one be introduced. When all possibility of passing a bill through elected officials is exhausted, citizens can start the initiative process.

Citizen sponsors research the state or local requirements for initiative petitions. The rules concerning the number of signatures and deadlines for submitting initiatives vary by jurisdiction. Consult the city or town clerk or registrar of voters for local rules. For a statewide petition, contact the secretary of state.

Sponsors must determine the exact wording of the new law, with the assistance of lawyers or legislators. Then the petition drive must be planned. The most effective petition drive strategy divides the total number of signatures required into manageable segments, either per volunteer, per month, or per week. Groups have to obtain at least 25 percent more signatures than the legal minimum to provide a cushion because officials will invalidate any illegible names and names of people not registered to vote in the jurisdiction.[130]

In most jurisdictions, sponsors are required to submit their petition to election officials before they start collecting signatures. After the petition has been circulated, sponsors submit the completed petition to election officials for verification and keep a receipt and photocopies of each petition in case it is lost by officials.[131]

COMMUNITY LAWYER

The residents of Winsted, Connecticut, have a community lawyer to help them exercise their rights and strengthen their involvement in the governance of their community. The lawyer serves as a watchdog and a representative of citizen interests at public meetings, helps citizens find the proper channels through which to make grievances known, refers citizens to useful sources of information, provides assistance with the technical aspects of introducing legislative initiatives to deal with specific concerns, and advocates on their behalf, pro bono, on issues of community wide significance.[132]

Charlene La Voie, the Winsted community lawyer drafted an ordinance to ban polystyrene foam food containers in Winsted. Despite strong opposition from plastics manufacturers and users, the town passed the ordinance, joining a growing number of communities across the country.[133]

The community lawyer has written pamphlets for citizens on freedom of information laws, the right of initiative, home rule, and local government to demystify the local and state government process. She writes, "Participatory government is not an efficient or tidy mode of governing. It requires that people assert their rights and accept their responsibilities as citizens. The [Community Lawyer] Project is one step toward strengthening the process and practice of self government."[134]

SHAREHOLDER ACTIVISM

Shareholder activism consists of filing shareholder resolutions and lobbying shareholders to vote in support of the resolutions, divesting of stock in unethical corporations, and investing in socially responsible enterprises. These techniques can generate publicity, educate corporate executives as well as the public, and shape the activities of corporations.[135]

Public corporations—those that sell stock to the public—hold annual meetings of shareholders to discuss the company's direction and to elect a new board of directors. Shareholders may vote on board nominees and on any resolutions dealing with company policy, including those proposed by shareholders.

Shareholders may file resolutions to be considered at the annual meeting. The federal Securities and Exchange Commission (SEC) oversees shareholder interaction with companies. The SEC has specific procedural requirements for shareholder resolutions.[136]

Because the management of a corporation generally controls a majority of the stock through proxies, it is nearly impossible to pass a shareholder resolution. About a third of the resolutions are never voted on because the company makes some concession on the issue and the resolution is withdrawn.[137] The purpose of most shareholder resolutions is to create publicity about corporate policy that would outrage the public enough to pressure legislators and corporate management to change policy.[138]

Shareholder activism techniques were first developed by community organizer Saul Alinsky, who in 1966 convinced the owners of 39,000 shares of Eastman Kodak to object to the management's record in hiring minorities.[139] Eventually, the company agreed to implement a minority hiring program.

The success of the South Africa divestment campaign is one example of effective shareholder activism. Throughout the 1970s and 1980s, a wide variety of religious, student, and citizen groups waged a campaign to force U.S. corporations to stop doing business in South Africa to protest that nation's policy of apartheid. Citizen groups filed shareholder resolutions and convinced large investors—including the state of California, the Smithsonian Institution, the cities of Washington and Philadelphia, and hundreds of churches, foundations, and state and city pension funds—to sell off their stock in companies that continued to operate in South Africa.[140] Students at more than 140 U.S. universities convinced their schools to adopt some divestment policy toward South Africa. Although the shareholder campaigns do not fully account for the divestment trend, between 1985 and 1988 some 172 U.S. companies ended their direct investment in South Africa.[141]

Many individual citizens, as well as institutional investors such as union pension funds, are investing their money in ethical or socially responsible companies; this gives investors more say about the use to which their investment funds are put.[142]

THE MEDIA: CITIZEN ACCESS TO NEWSPAPERS, TELEVISION, AND RADIO*

Access to the media—newspapers, television, and radio—is an important way to reach the public with your group's message. The following information applies to university newspapers and radio stations as well as local, state, and national media.

Letters to the Editor

Americans read the letters column more frequently than anything else on the editorial page.[143] Letters are therefore an extremely effective way to air different points of view on an issue. Of course, newspapers do not print every letter received, but many papers tabulate letters for in-house opinion surveys.[144]

To increase the chances that the paper prints your letter, follow these guidelines.

- Keep it short and on target to avoid having it edited. Newspapers may cut a long letter down to 250 words or less.

- Avoid flowery language and unnecessary lead-ins such as "I'm sure everyone would agree with me that . . ."

- Make reference to a recent editorial column or news story that prompted your letter.

- Send an original, neat, handwritten or preferably, typed letter. Newspapers reject photocopied letters but may print letters from an organized letter-writing campaign if each letter is original.

* Much of the discussion of the media, unless otherwise indicated, is derived from Marc Caplan, *A Citizens' Guide to Lobbying*, (New York: Dembner Books, 1983) 84-101.

Op-Ed Articles

In addition to letters, papers run opinion columns on the editorial or opposite editorial page or both. The writers for large-circulation papers usually are nationally syndicated columnists, and newspapers may give little space to articles on local matters written by local citizens. Ask your paper what its policy is concerning opinion columns submitted by local citizens. Most university papers dedicate the op-ed page to student views.

Citizen Responses to Editorials

Radio and television stations often broadcast editorials. The Federal Communications Commission abolished the Fairness Doctrine in 1987, lifting a requirement that broadcasters present differing points of view. However, some broadcasters do welcome responses from citizens. This is an excellent way to explain your view on an issue without any interruption or editing by a reporter or news editor.

WRC-TV in Washington, D.C., airs station editorials and responses from the community on controversial local issues. The station also broadcasts "Your Turn," a program that gives citizens an opportunity to address the community about issues of their own choosing. Challenge your local stations to provide similar opportunities for citizen access.

Feature Stories

Feature stories, in print or on television, are best suited to a description of an interesting personality or a special activity. If your group has a good subject for a feature story, let appropriate newspersons know.

Editorial Endorsements

The editorial support of the local or university newspaper can carry tremendous weight for a particular issue or for your organization. Present your case to the editor. If the paper thinks that your proposal is a good one or that your actions are constructive, it is harder for others in the community to attack you as irresponsible without somehow implying that the paper also is wrong.

Weekly Columns

Whereas it is often difficult to get space in a daily paper, certain weekly papers, especially local shoppers, can be a good place to start a column by you or your organization. Daily papers may be willing to run a well-written guest column occasionally.

Call-in Shows

Many radio stations have talk lines on which listeners may call in to discuss a variety of issues. Calling in your views on an issue can do much to broaden public awareness, reaching thousands of people.

Guest Shows

Guest shows and panel shows on local radio and television stations are important platforms for reaching large numbers of people. It is often difficult to arrange a booking on one of these shows, but the more you and your issues are publicized, the more likely your request will be granted. Make sure that the people who select interviewees or panelists know whom you represent and the importance of what you and your group are doing.

Public Service Announcements

Many radio and television stations air public service announcements (PSAs). This is free time reserved for announcing events and meetings or for providing public service information. It cannot be used to denounce a legislator, advocate legislation, or otherwise express an opinion.

Call local television and radio stations to find out their procedures for accepting PSAs, including standard length, whether they prefer a written script or a prepared tape, and the deadline for submission.

News Releases

Use news or press releases to announce events that are newsworthy but would not receive coverage without a release. Write press releases in a clear, concise news style. Write the release as you would like to see it appear in the paper. Read the paper closely, and write your story so that it sounds like one of the articles you have just read. You or your group should be referred to in the third person, for example, "Students for the Environment announced today . . ." To express an opinion, use direct quotations, and identify the sources.

Make the major point of the story clearly and directly in the first paragraph. For the rest of the release, follow the inverted pyramid style: the most vital information at the beginning of the release, with subsequent paragraphs arranged in order of declining importance. Newspaper writers use this style to allow editors to cut the story from the bottom, leaving the most important information. Include a brief description of the group.

Start the release with the group's name, address, and telephone number at the top of the page, or use official stationery. In addition, at the top of the release, give the name of a specific person who can answer questions. Use a headline, just like a newspaper story. For releases of more than one page, write "MORE" at the end of each page except the last. On the last page, type "###" or "-30-" under the final paragraph to mark the end of the release (see Figure 3).

Keep the following points in mind.

- If you live in a city with both a morning and evening newspaper, try to divide releases evenly between them to avoid alienating either paper.

- Less official news happens on weekends and holidays than during the workweek. Delivering on Thursday or Friday for release on

Sample News Release

Students for the Environment
City University
Anytown, USA 00000
(000) 555-1111

NEWS RELEASE

FOR RELEASE: CONTACT: Jane Doe
January 3, 1994, 10:00 A.M.   Tel.: 555-1111

Students Find City University Wasting Energy

Student environmentalists conducted an energy waste hunt at City University in Anytown and found wasteful energy practices. "City University is throwing taxpayer money out the window as well as disregarding the environmental costs of wasting energy," said Jane Doe, president of Students for the Environment, the group that conducted the survey.

The waste hunt found the following: students in classrooms in the Arts Department building open windows in cold weather due to a malfunctioning thermostat that causes too much heat in those classrooms; the heating and air-conditioning equipment has not been serviced in three years; and dirty, dusty lighting fixtures cause students and professors to turn on more lighting than would be necessary if the fixtures were clean.

"The changes we are proposing cost little, and the potential savings on energy bills are big," said Doe.

The group asked the university administration to implement the following changes: replace the thermostat in the Arts Department building; implement regular servicing of heating and cooling equipment, including cleaning and replacing filters; clean lighting fixtures; consider buying heat pumps to help the furnaces operate more efficiently (heat pumps can cut electricity use by 30 to 40 percent, according to the U.S. Department of Energy); and establish a student energy task force to continue monitoring wasteful energy practices.

Students for the Environment plans to track City University's utility bills over the next few months to measure savings from the changes.

Students for the Environment, formed in 1991, is a group of 300 students at City University who have joined together to promote energy efficiency, recycling, and other environmental issues.

###

weekends or holidays is sometimes a good way to ensure more coverage. Monday morning papers are especially in need of news because few staff people collect news over the weekend.

- Take advantage of seasonal lulls—during the summer or around holidays. Be aware, however, that the audience can be smaller at those times.

- Wednesday papers usually carry a great deal of advertising—mainly supermarket ads. More ads mean more pages and usually more space for news.

- Do not assume special knowledge on the part of the press. Although members of the press may be able to grasp your issues and arguments better than the general public, they are seldom experts on all the issues they cover.

News Conferences

Use news conferences for events that are urgent and important. News conferences are particularly welcomed by radio and television stations and serve several purposes, such as initiating a major project, announcing the conclusions of a study, exposing injustices, or calling for a ban on a harmful product.

Limit news conferences to significant statements or events. The quickest way to diminish your overall press coverage, especially with radio and television reporters, is to call news conferences too often.

The key to a successful conference is careful planning so that everything runs smoothly. For example, be sure that the podium and microphone are at the correct height for the speaker and that all electronic equipment is in proper working order.

Here are a few specific things to keep in mind when planning a news conference.

- Prepare and rehearse the conference thoroughly, ahead of time.

- The day before your conference, issue an editor's advisory over the local wire services—Associated Press (AP) and United Press International (UPI)—announcing the time and place of the conference and the general topic. To issue the advisory, call your local AP and UPI offices and say that you have an item to be listed in their daybook. Keep the advisory short. Mentioning visuals is especially important to attract television cameras. Provide a telephone number and the name of a person to call for additional information. But do not go into too great detail about your announcements or subject matter to avoid giving away the main news of the conference.

- Call radio and television stations early on the morning of the conference as a reminder. Talk with the assignment editor or news director. Give the pertinent data, and do a brief selling job.

- Send both the newspaper's assignment editor and the reporter covering your issue an advisory several days before the conference and call them again the day before the conference, Point out any scheduled visual event so that they can send a photographer.

- Make the location for the conference as easily accessible as possible. If the location has to be out of the way, provide directions in your editor's advisory or phone calls.

- If the location is outdoors, have an alternative indoor site in case of bad weather. Make your decision to move the conference in time to give the press adequate notice.

- Most news conferences consist of a statement from the speaker followed by questions from the press.

- Deliver copies of any materials to be distributed at the conference to the wire services a few hours before the conference. Local wire service bureaus usually do not cover news conferences because of insufficient staff. Most radio stations and many local newspapers get their news from the wire services, so be sure that the wire services receive all materials released. Materials delivered before the news conference should be marked "Embargo," to alert reporters to wait until the start of the news conference to report the information.

- Have your release ready to hand out at the conference. The release should begin with the major point or issue of your conference, not with the fact that you are having a conference.

Media Events

Use media events to dramatize a point that would not receive attention otherwise. Media events with a large number of people or a degree of flamboyance are often most effective. Pickets, marches, rallies, and displays are some common media events. Many citizen groups have developed creative events that depend less on large numbers of people and more on uniqueness.[145] For example, when Public Citizen was lobbying Congress for air bag safety protection in automobiles, Public Citizen president Joan Claybrook arranged to have crash-damaged cars parked next to the U.S. Capitol with the owners of the cars, who survived the crashes only because the cars had been equipped with experimental air bags, standing nearby.[146]

Radio Interviews

Here are some suggestions for handling radio audios.

- Ask for the newsroom, identify yourself and your group, and say you have a news story. If no one is available in the newsroom, leave a message and call back periodically.

- Prepare a summary of the news release. Have an outline of important points before you.

- Be prepared to answer typical questions, such as "What is the significance of this survey?" or "What does your group want public officials to do?"

- When the station is taping, the phone will sound as if it is dead except for the "beep" some stations use when recording.

- If you make a factual error, tell the interviewer; it is easy to retape and much better than putting a mistake on the air. Remember also that pauses and stumbling can be edited out.

- Finally, if the interviewer says something inaccurate, do not hesitate to break in politely and make a correction. Remember that most interviewers are trying to cooperate with you to produce a good story.

Basics for Better Coverage

To use the news media effectively and maximize your coverage, Marc Caplan makes the following suggestions.

- Your story must be action-oriented and timely. Something must happen—something that will interest the public.

- If you want television coverage, make your story visual.

- Include a positive call for action. An approach that consists of attacking without ever advancing some positive action is not popular.

- The various media face different time constraints. Reporters for afternoon papers may need material by 8:30 A.M. to make the first edition. Television people often need their information by 3:00 P.M. for the evening news. Learn the deadlines for papers and broadcasts, and consider these deadlines when you release a story.

- Prepare a standard press list, including national, state, and local newspapers, wire services, radio and television stations, and relevant magazines. Include the name of the editor or news director for each, along with other contacts, such as reporters or people who might have a special interest in your story. Also include editorial writers on the list. Make up address labels and photocopy them onto labels or keep a computerized mailing list to save the time of typing envelopes each time you send out a release.

- Deliver releases by hand or by facsimile machine (fax) to local news outlets. When the release is dropped off in person, better coverage often results if you have an opportunity to talk to an editor or a reporter and explain the importance of your story.

- Whenever you put out a report longer than a few pages or longer than ten minutes' reading, issue a brief summary as well as the press release.

- Joint or coalition releases can maximize coverage of your issue. Ask other groups to endorse your position either one at a time or simultaneously. Discretion is advisable here; you may not want to be associated with every organization.

FUNDRAISING*

From a university club to a nationwide citizen group, almost all organizations need money to carry out their programs and activities. Fundraising options include dues, pledges, door-to-door canvassing, direct mail, payroll deductions, special events, grants, and selling newsletters, products, or services.

Dues produce a dependable income for programs. Joan Flanagan, author of *The Grass Roots Fundraising Book,* suggests that to set up a dues rate, figure out how much money is needed for a program and then divide by the number of people who will realistically buy memberships. This should approximate the amount a membership should cost. Many groups offer memberships that vary according to income to allow more people to join. For example, many groups provide lower rates for senior citizens, students, and others who live on a fixed income.

Pledges provide the opportunity to spread a donation over a period of time. For example, a contributor may give $10 per month for twelve months instead of giving $120 up front. Pledges offer flexibility for people on limited incomes who still want to make a large contribution.

Door-to-door canvassing is the most labor-intensive form of fundraising but can also produce the highest profits for the organization. The work is difficult, so usually canvassers are paid by either commissions or salary. Groups that are wellknown or located in a large city often use a professional canvassing service; smaller community groups often canvass with volunteers. Canvassing also provides instant feedback on public opinion about your projects.

Direct mail—sending an appeal to prospective donors or members through the mail—is expensive and usually results in only a small percentage of responses. However, if appeals are sent to enough people, even a small percentage can result in many new dues-paying members. Direct-mail expenses include postage, stationery, and envelopes. Special postage rates exist for mass mailings and for mailings by groups with nonprofit status.

Newsletters are an effective way to tell people about activities and specific programs as well as to bring in money from subscription charges and advertisements.

Special events—speakers' bureaus, dances, potluck dinners, holiday or seasonal carnivals, raffles—are important ways to build community

---

* Much of the discussion of fundraising, unless otherwise noted, is derived from Joan Flanagan, *The Grassroots Fundraising Book: How to Raise Money in Your Community,* 2nd rev. ed. (Chicago: Contemporary Books, 1982).

support and involvement as well as raise money. Operating a business such as a thrift shop or used-book store or providing a service are also good ways to raise money.

The Buffalo, New York, affiliate of Women's Action for Nuclear Disarmament (WAND) organizes a "Mums for Moms" flower sale every Mother's Day. The flowers come with a peace message and information about the organization. WAND has a kit to help other groups organize similar sales.[147]

Obtaining Grants

Pursuing grants from the government, foundations, or corporations is a highly competitive way to raise funds. In addition, grant makers may impose restrictions on how the money can be used, inhibiting the organization's freedom to make its own decisions. Many foundations are willing to provide start-up or seed money with the understanding that the group will become self-sufficient.[148] Research funding sources thoroughly to determine the conditions for grants; many give only within a specific geographical or issue area. To locate foundations, consult the *Grant Seekers Guide, The Foundation Directory*, and contact the Foundation Center, which maintains collections of materials in over one hundred U.S. cities.[149]

Many citizen groups apply to the Internal Revenue Service (IRS) for tax-exempt status either under Section 501(c)(3) or Section 501(c)(4) of the IRS Code. To qualify under Internal Revenue Code Section 501(c)(3) for tax-exempt status, an organization must be a "nonprofit corporation, unincorporated association, or trust which engages in educational, religious, scientific or other charitable activities."[150] Such organizations may accept contributions from individuals and corporations, which are deductible from the donor's federal income tax. Organizations with 501(c)(3) status may accept funding from foundations. The lobbying activities of 501(c)(3) organizations are restricted, and such organizations may not engage in partisan political campaign activities. State laws governing nonprofit organizations vary.

An organization that qualifies for tax-exempt status under the Internal Revenue Code Section 501(c)(4) must be "designed to develop and implement programs for the promotion of 'social welfare.'"[151] Although 501(c)(4) organizations are exempt from paying federal taxes, contributors and members may not deduct contributions or dues from their own federal income tax. A 501(c)(4) organization is not limited in its lobbying activities, may advocate a point of view on controversial issues, and may engage in limited political campaign activities. The Internal Revenue Service publishes a free pamphlet explaining tax-exempt status.[152]

Writing a Grant Proposal

Although the requirements for each foundation and government agency vary widely, the following guidelines are a good starting point for writing a grant proposal.[153]

- Begin with a clear, concise summary to describe the group, the scope of its project, and the projected costs. Grant makers appreciate proposal summaries.

- Follow the summary with an introduction to establish the organization's history, credibility, uniqueness, significant accomplishments, and goals. Follow the introduction with a problem statement or an assessment of need. Establish the program objectives. Describe the project's goals and how the project will accomplish them.

- Include a detailed budget. Ask for a specific amount of money. Establish that, once the grant ends, the group will be able to continue the program without the funding source.

- After sending the proposal, follow up with a phone call. Ask whether the foundation received the proposal and if it has any questions or needs additional materials.

For more information on foundations and grant writing, consult *Foundation Fundamentals* and *Securing Your Organization's Future.*[154]

RESOURCES

Children's Advocacy Organizations

Advocates for Children of New York, Inc.
24-16 Bridge Plaza South
Long Island City, NY 11101
Works to protect educational entitlements and due process rights of disadvantaged public school children in New York City. Publishes The Advocate *four times a year.*

Children Now
926 J Street, Suite 1400
Sacramento, CA 95814
Combines policy analysis, outreach, implementation, and advocacy strategies to improve the lives of children and their families. Publishes the annual Report Card *grading the condition of California's children.*

Children's Defense Fund
25 E Street, N.W.
Washington, DC 20001
Conducts research and advocacy on behalf of poor, minority, and disabled children. Publishes Adolescent Pregnancy Prevention Clearinghouse *six times a year and* Children's Defense Fund Reports *monthly.*

Citizenship and Legal Education Organizations

American Bar Association
750 North Lake Shore Drive
Chicago, IL 60611
A nonprofit, independent national research institute committed to basic research on law and legal institutions. Publishes law-related educational materials.

Center for Civic Education
5146 Douglas Fir Road
Calabasas, CA 91302
Works to improve educational resources and curricula for civics education. Publishes Center Correspondent *quarterly.*

Center for Research and Development in Law-Related Education (CRADLE)
Wake Forest University School of Law
2714 Henning Drive
Winston-Salem, NC 27106
Promotes effective citizenship through innovative strategies created by teachers for teachers. Publishes SPLICE Newsletter *and* LRE Bridge Newsletter.

Close Up Foundation
44 Canal Center Plaza
Alexandria, VA 22314
A nonpartisan educational foundation promoting citizen involvement in government.

Connecticut Consortium for Law and Citizenship Education
Office of the Secretary of State
30 Trinity Street
Hartford, CT 06106
Promotes law and citizenship education in Connecticut schools.

Constitutional Rights Foundation (CRF)
601 South Kingsley Drive
Los Angeles, CA 90005
Publishes School Youth Service Network, *a quarterly newsletter that reports on youth service projects around the country and the progress of statewide community service programs.*

National Institute for Citizen Education in the Law (NICEL)
711 G Street, S.E.
Washington, DC 20003
Educates citizens on the law and the U.S. legal system.

Ohio Center for Law-Related Education
1700 Lake Shore Drive
Columbus, OH 43204
Works to advance citizenship education in Ohio.

Civil Rights and Civil Liberties Organizations

American-Arab Anti-Discrimination Committee
4201 Connecticut Avenue, N.W., Suite 500
Washington, DC 20008
Works to combat anti-Arab stereotyping, defamation and discrimination and to promote a better understanding of the cultural heritage of Arab Americans. Publishes ADC Times, *newsletter ten times a year.*

American Civil Liberties Union
132 West 43rd Street, 2nd floor
New York, NY 10036
Works to protect and expand the rights and liberties of U.S. citizens and to defend the U.S. Constitution through litigation.

Human Rights Campaign Fund
1012 14th Street, N.W., Suite 607
Washington, DC 20005
Committed to securing full civil rights for lesbians and gay men and responsible federal policies on AIDS. Mobilizes grassroots support

and lobbies, educates, and helps elect legislators who support the goals of equality for the community. Publishes Momentum *quarterly.*

Lambda Legal Defense and Education Fund, Inc.
666 Broadway, 12th floor
New York, NY 10012
Pursues test-case litigation nationwide in areas of concern to gay men and lesbians. Publishes AIDS Update *six times a year and* Lambda Update *three times a year.*

Leadership Conference on Civil Rights
1629 K Street, N.W., Suite 1010
Washington, DC 20006
Consisting of 185 national organizations, serves as the legislative arm of the civil rights movement.

Mexican American Legal Defense and Educational Fund (MALDEF)
634 South Spring Street, 11th floor
Los Angeles, CA 90014
Works to protect the civil rights of Hispanic Americans through class action litigation, advocacy, and community education. Publishes MALDEF Newsletter *three times a year.*

National Association for the Advancement of Colored People (NAACP)
4805 Mount Hope Drive
Baltimore, MD 21215
Works to ensure the political, educational, social and economic equality of African Americans primarily through litigation and lobbying. Publishes CRISIS Magazine *monthly.*

National Gay and Lesbian Task Force
1734 14th Street, N.W.
Washington, DC 20009
Uses lobbying and citizen organizing to work for gay and lesbian civil rights and a responsive federal AIDS policy. Publishes annual Gay Violence and Victimization Report *and* Task Force Report *quarterly.*

National Indian Education Association
1819 H Street, N.W., Suite 800
Washington, DC 20006
Helps Native American and Alaskan Native students keep traditional tribal values while learning to be productive citizens in an increasingly technological world.

National Rainbow Coalition
1700 K Street, N.W., Suite 800
Washington, DC 20006

Works to empower, advocate, persuade and build consensus in the areas of civil rights, religion, labor, government, education, business, academia, the environment, and health care.

National Urban League
500 East 62nd Street
New York, NY 10021
Works to promote educational attainment, employment, and economic self-sufficiency for African Americans. Publishes Urban League News *quarterly.*

Native American Rights Fund
1506 Broadway
Boulder, CO 80302
Works on issues related to the preservation of tribal existence, protection of tribal natural resources, promotion of human rights, government accountability, and the development of Native American law.

Operation PUSH (People United to Serve Humanity)
930 East 50th Street
Chicago, IL 60615
Works to revitalize African-American communities.

Puerto Rican Legal Defense and Education Fund
99 Hudson Street, 14th floor
New York, NY 10013
Works to protect Puerto Ricans and other Latinos in areas such as education, fair housing, employment discrimination, voting rights, and health care.

Southern Christian Leadership Conference (SCLC)
334 Auburn Avenue, N.E.
Atlanta, GA 30312
Works to provide moral and spiritual leadership in the struggle against racial oppression. Publishes SCLC Magazine *four to six times a year.*

Southern Poverty Law Center
400 Washington Avenue
Montgomery, AL 36195
Operates the Klanwatch Project to monitor the activities of and file suit against illegal white supremacist activities. Publishes Teaching Tolerance, *a biannual publication to help teachers promote racial and religious tolerance in the classroom.*

Community Lawyer

Charlene La Voie
P.O. Box 1044
Winchester, CT 06098

Association of Community Organizations for Reform Now (ACORN)
845 Flatbush Avenue
Brooklyn, NY 11226
With offices in several cities, organizes people in low-income communities to work on campaigns involving such issues as housing, banking, and education.

Citizen Action
1120 19th Street, N.W., Suite 630
Washington, DC 20036
A national citizens' political organization dedicated to increasing citizen participation in economic and political decision making. Publishes Citizen Action News *quarterly.*

Midwest Academy
225 West Ohio Street, Suite 250
Chicago, IL 60610
Works to help low- and moderate-income people win benefits and empower themselves to build a more just society.

National Association of Neighborhoods (NAN)
1651 Fuller Street, N.W.
Washington, DC 20009
Consists of over two thousand community groups and small businesses working to promote social and economic development. Publishes NAN Bulletin *quarterly.*

National People's Action
810 North Milwaukee Avenue
Chicago, IL 60622
A nationwide network of grassroots community activists who work on a variety of issues.

Consumer and Corporate Accountability Organizations

Action for Corporate Accountability
129 Church Street
New Haven, CT 06510
Alerts the public and takes action to stop corporate practices that cause infant death and disease. Conducts a boycott of Nestlé and American Home Products for violations of international infant formula standards. Publishes Action News *newsletter three times a year.*

American Association of Retired Persons (AARP)
601 E Street, N.W.
Washington, DC 20049

Serves the needs and interests of retired persons through legislative advocacy, research, informative programs, and community services. Publishes Modern Maturity *magazine monthly.*

Bankcard Holders of America
560 Herndon Parkway, Suite 120
Herndon, VA 22070
Educates the public about the wise and careful use of credit.

Buyers Up
P.O. Box 53005
Washington, DC 20009
A membership organization dedicated to saving people money through group purchases of heating oil and energy services. Publishes Buyers Up News *quarterly.*

Center for Auto Safety
2001 S Street, N.W., Suite 410
Washington, DC 20009
Conducts research and advocacy on highway safety and vehicle safety, economy, and reliability and informs citizens of consumer transportation issues. Publishes Impact *bimonthly and* The Lemon Times *quarterly.*

Center for the Study of Commercialism
1875 Connecticut Avenue, N.W., Suite 300
Washington, DC 20009
Researches, documents, publicizes, and opposes the excessive intrusion of commercial interests in society. Publishes Advice *newsletter.*

Consumer Action
116 New Montgomery Street, Suite 223
San Francisco, CA 94105
Works to educate and advise the public through a telephone consumer line, publications, and public hearings. Publishes The CA Newsletter *eight times a year.*

Consumer Federation of America
1424 16th Street, N.W., Suite 604
Washington, DC 20036
An advocacy, education, and membership organization that works to advance pro-consumer policy before Congress, regulatory agencies, and the courts. Publishes CFAnews *eight times a year.*

Consumers Union
256 Washington Street
Mount Vernon, NY 10553
Provides consumers with information and advice on goods, services, health, personal finance, and a variety of other consumer issues. Publishes Consumer Reports *monthly.*

Co-op America
1850 M Street, N.W., Suite 700
Washington, DC 20036
Promotes consumer cooperatives and educates consumers and businesses on socially responsible buying and investing. Publishes Co-op America *quarterly and* Boycott Action News *quarterly.*

FairTest, National Center for Fair and Open Testing
342 Broadway
Cambridge, MA 02139
Works to end the abuses, misuses, and flaws of standardized testing. Publishes FairTest Examiner *newsletter quarterly.*

Government Purchasing Project
P.O. Box 19367
Washington, DC 20036
Promotes government purchase and use of energy-efficient and environmentally sound technologies and products.

INFACT
256 Hanover Street, 3rd floor
Boston, MA 02113
Works on international campaigns to stop the abuses of transnational corporations that endanger the health and survival of people around the world. Publishes INFACT Campaign Update *three or four times a year.*

Institute for Consumer Responsibility (ICR)
6506 28th Avenue, N.E.
Seattle, WA 98115
Educates citizens to exercise direct control over corporations by using the boycott for social change. Publishes National Boycott News.

Interfaith Center on Corporate Responsibility (ICCR)
475 Riverside Drive, Room 566
New York, NY 10115
Helps members work as institutional investors to hold corporations socially accountable. Publishes The Corporate Examiner *ten times a year.*

National Consumers League (NCL)
815 15th Street, N.W., Suite 928
Washington, DC 20005
Conducts research, education, and advocacy to represent and inform consumers and workers. Publishes NCL Bulletin *bimonthly.*

National Insurance Consumer Organization
121 Payne Street
Alexandria, VA 22314
Educates consumers on all aspects of buying insurance and serves as a consumer advocate on public policy matters.

Public Citizen
2000 P Street, N.W.
Washington, DC 20036
An umbrella organization for Buyers Up, Litigation Group, Health Research Group, and Congress Watch that works to protect and promote the rights of consumers and citizens.

United States Public Interest Research Group (U.S. PIRG)
215 Pennsylvania Avenue, S.E.
Washington, DC 20003
The national lobbying office for state PIRGs. Focuses on environmental and consumer protection and energy and government reform. Publishes Citizen Agenda *quarterly.*

Virginia Citizens Consumer Council
7115 Leesburg Pike, Suite 215
Falls Church, VA 22043
Promotes and represents the rights and general interests of consumers. Publishes bi-monthly newsletter VCCC Voice.

Voter Revolt
3325 Wilshire Boulevard, Suite 550
Los Angeles, CA 90010
Works to change the role and influence of citizens in lawmaking by advocating reform measures of critical concern to Californians.

Education Organizations

FairTest, National Center for Fair and Open Testing
342 Broadway
Cambridge, MA 02139
Works to eliminate the biases and inadequacies of national tests at all grade levels. Publishes FairTest Examiner *quarterly.*

Highlander Research and Education Center
Route 3, Box 370
New Market, TN 37820
Works to help communities deal with the structural causes of economic, environmental, and social problems in a democratic, practical, and effective manner. Publishes Highlander Reports *newsletter quarterly.*

LULAC National Educational Service Centers
777 North Capitol Street, N.E., Suite 305
Washington, DC 20002
Works with business and government to improve the educational conditions of the Latino community in the United States. Publishes Opportunity to Lead *three times a year.*

National Council for History Education, Inc.
26915 Westwood Road, Suite A-2
Westlake, OH 44145
Promotes the importance of history in school and society. Publishes
History Matters! *ten times a year.*

National Issues Forums
200 Commons Road
Dayton, OH 45459
Holds public forums around the country aimed at increasing citizen discussion and cultivating the art of public debate about the issues of the day.

People for the American Way
2000 M Street, N.W., Suite 400
Washington, DC 20036
Promotes constitutional liberties such as First Amendment rights and the right to privacy and civil rights through education, advocacy, and litigation. Publishes Right Wing Watch, *a quarterly newsletter.*

Project Public Life
Hubert H. Humphrey Institute of Public Affairs
301 19th Avenue South
Minneapolis, MN 55455
Works to stimulate discussion on public decision making and has a program of citizen education in the use of power, judgment, imagination, and reflection on experience.

Study Circle Resource Center
Route 169, Box 203
Pomfret, CT 06258
Publishes course material and articles for small-group discussions around issues and themes of democracy and citizenship.

Elderly Organizations

American Association of Retired Persons (AARP)
601 E Street, N.W.
Washington, DC 20049
Serves the needs and interests of retired persons through legislative advocacy, research, information programs, and community services. Publishes Modern Maturity *magazine monthly.*

Gray Panthers
2025 Pennsylvania Avenue, N.W.
Washington, DC 20006
An intergenerational organization working on issues of peace and social justice that affect people of all ages. Publishes a bi-annual newspaper and a newsletter eight times a year.

National Council of Senior Citizens
925 15th Street, N.W.
Washington, DC 20005
Advocates on behalf of senior citizens. Publishes Senior Citizen
News.

Environmental Organizations

Acid Rain Foundation
1410 Varsity Drive
Raleigh, NC 27606
Provides educational materials on acid rain for grades K-12.

Bio-Integral Resource Center
P.O. Box 7414
Berkeley, CA 94707
*Provides information on the least toxic methods of managing pests.
Publishes* IPM Practitioner *and* Common Sense Pest Control
newsletter quarterly.

California Rural Legal Assistance Foundation/Earth Island
Institute
2111 Mission Street, Suite 401
San Francisco, CA 94110
*Provides free legal service to low-income people in California. Pub-
lishes* El Noticiero *newsletter monthly.*

Center for the Biology of Natural Systems
Queens College, City University of New York
Flushing, NY 11367
*Researches municipal solid-waste disposal, renewable energy, and
other environmental issues.*

Central States Education Center
809 South Fifth Street
Champaign, IL 61820
*Helps citizen groups work to protect their local environment by
offering technical assistance on waste issues.*

Citizens Clearinghouse for Hazardous Waste (CCHW)
119 Rowell Court
Falls Church, VA 22040
*Helps local group formation; and fights dumps, incinerators, toxic
discharges, military waste, and other forms of toxic pollution.
Publishes* Everyone's Backyard *bimonthly and* Environmental
Health *monthly.*

Clean Water Action Project
1320 18th Street, N.W., Suite 300
Washington, DC 20036

Works for clean and safe water, controlling toxic chemicals, and the protection of natural resources. Publishes Clean Water Action News.

Concern, Inc.
1794 Columbia Road, N.W.
Washington, DC 20009
Provides environmental information and guidelines for community action.

Council on Economic Priorities
30 Irving Place
New York, NY 10003
Works to enhance corporate performance in the areas of military spending, energy, the environment, and fair employment practices.

Council on the Environment of New York City (CENYC)
51 Chambers Street, Room 228
New York, NY 10007
Works to promote environmental awareness among New Yorkers and to develop solutions to environmental problems.

Ecology Center
2530 San Pablo Avenue
Berkeley, CA 94702
Provides information on recycling, ecology, nature, environment, gardening, and farming. Publishes monthly newsletter Vegetable Gardening.

Environmental Action Coalition
625 Broadway, 2nd floor
New York, NY 10012
Works on solid waste, urban forestry, water use, and environmental education issues. Publishes Cycle newsletter quarterly.

Environmental Action Foundation
6930 Carroll Avenue, Suite 600
Takoma Park, MD 20912
Works on issues such as acid rain, plastics, solid waste, and toxics through research, public education, organizing, advocacy, and legal action. Publishes Environmental Action Magazine and Powerline bimonthly and Wastelines quarterly.

Environmental Defense Fund
257 Park Avenue South
New York, NY 10010
Links science, economics, and law to create economically viable solutions to environmental problems.

Environmental Health Watch
4115 Bridge Avenue, Suite 104
Cleveland, OH 44113
*An information center on hazardous materials in the home and
community, designed to educate the public on the health effects of
dangerous toxics.*

Environmental Research Foundation
P.O. Box 5036
Annapolis, MD 21403
*Provides technical assistance to citizens facing toxic problems.
Publishes* Rachel's Hazardous Waste News Weekly.

Friends of the Earth
218 D Street, S.E.
Washington, DC 20003
*Works with hundreds of grassroots groups on issues ranging from
groundwater protection and agricultural biotechnology to prevention of toxic chemical accidents. Publishes* Friends of the Earth
newsletter monthly.

Global Tomorrow Coalition
1325 G Street, N.W., Suite 1010
Washington, DC 20005
*Works to build U.S. leadership on long-term, interrelated trends in
environment, population, and resource use.*

Greenpeace
1436 U Street, N.W.
Washington, DC 20009
*Conducts campaigns on toxic waste elimination, nuclear disarma-
ment, protection of marine mammals, and alternatives to environmentally destructive energy consumption. Publishes* Greenpeace
quarterly.

Household Hazardous Waste Project
1031 East Battlefield, Suite 214
Springfield, MO 65807
*Provides training, educational, and organizing materials for its
clearinghouse and referral service, answering questions regarding
household hazardous materials.*

INFORM, Inc.
381 Park Avenue South
New York, NY 10016
*Researches such issues as hazardous waste reduction, garbage man-
agement, air pollution, and land and water conservation. Publishes* INFORM Reports *quarterly.*

Institute for Local Self-Reliance
2425 18th Street, N.W.
Washington, DC 20009
Encourages cities to pursue local self-reliance as a development strategy, combining local political authority and modern technology to become more independent.

Kids Against Pollution
Tenakill High School
275 High Street
Closter, NJ 07624
Antipollution organization run by and for students.

National Coalition Against the Misuse of Pesticides (NCAMP)
530 Seventh Street, S.E.
Washington, DC 20003
Researches and publishes information on alternatives to pesticides. Publishes Pesticides and You *four times a year and* The Technical Report, *a monthly four page news brief.*

National Library of Medicine
U.S. Department of Health and Human Services
TRI Representative
8600 Rockville Pike
Bethesda, MD 20894
Manages the TOXNET system, which includes the Toxic Release Inventory database.

National Recycling Coalition, Inc. (NRC)
1101 30th Street, N.W., Suite 305
Washington, DC 20007
Association of professional recyclers, environmental groups, and individuals. Promotes recycling and provides technical assistance and information on recycling. Publishes The NRC Connection *quarterly.*

National Toxics Campaign
P.O. Box 206
Allston, MA 02134
Works to implement citizen-based preventive solutions to toxic and environmental problems. Publishes Toxic Times: Right-to-Know News *quarterly.*

National Wildlife Federation
1400 16th Street, N.W.
Washington, DC 20036
Promotes the wise use of natural resources and the protection of the global environment. Publishes Cool It! Connection *quarterly.*

Natural Resources Defense Council
40 West 20th Street
New York, NY 10011
Works to protect America's endangered natural resources by monitoring and working with government agencies, scientific research, litigation, and citizen education. Publishes AMICUS Journal.

Nature Conservancy
1815 North Lynn Street
Arlington, VA 22209
International environmental organization dedicated to the preservation of global diversity (rare plants, animals, and natural communities). Publishes The Nature Conservancy *bimonthly.*

New York Public Interest Research Group (NYPIRG)
9 Murray Street
New York, NY 10007
A student-run statewide environmental and consumer organization working on solid-waste issues, nuclear power, and incineration.

Nuclear Information and Resource Service
1424 16th Street, N.W., Suite 601
Washington, DC 20036
A national clearinghouse and networking center on nuclear power issues. Publishes The Nuclear Monitor *biweekly.*

OMB Watch
1731 Connecticut Avenue, N.W., 4th Floor
Washington, DC 20009
Monitors the Office of Management and Budget, the largest unit within the Executive Office of the President. Provides citizen education on related legislative and administrative issues. Publishes OMB Watcher *newsletter bimonthly.*

Rainforest Action Network
450 Sansome, Suite 700
San Francisco, CA 94111
Coordinates environmental and human rights organizations on major campaigns to protect the rainforests. Publishes Action Alert *monthly and* World Rainforest Report *quarterly.*

Renew America
1400 16th Street, N.W., Suite 710
Washington, DC 20036
An environmental education organization researching positive local, state, and national policies and programs designed to protect and enhance the environment.

Rocky Mountain Institute (RMI)
1739 Snowmass Creek Road
Old Snowmass, CO 81654
*Researches energy, water, agriculture, economic renewal, and global
energy issues to encourage an efficient and sustainable use of
resources as a path to global security. Publishes* RMI Newsletter.

Safe Energy Communication Council (SECC)
1717 Massachusetts Avenue, N.W., Suite 805
Washington, DC 20036
*A national coalition of environmental, energy, and media groups
working to increase public awareness on energy efficiency and
renewable energy.*

Save What's Left
Coral Springs High School
7201 West Sample Road
Coral Springs, FL 33065
*A worldwide network of high school students working on a variety of
environmental issues.*

Sierra Club
730 Polk Street
San Francisco, CA 94109
*Works on enforcement of the Clean Air Act, preserving national parks
and forests, global warming, and international development
lending reform. Publishes* Sierra *magazine monthly and* National
News Report *26 times a year.*

Student Environmental Action Coalition
University of North Carolina
P.O. Box 1168
Chapel Hill, NC 27514
*An alliance of student environmental organizations that acts as a
clearinghouse of information and facilitates the sharing of knowl-
edge and experience necessary to achieve a healthy planet.*

Union of Concerned Scientists
26 Church Street
Cambridge, MA 02238
*A nonprofit organization of nearly 100,000 scientists and other
citizens concerned about the impact of advanced technology,
including nuclear power, on society. Publishes* Nucleus *magazine
quarterly and* The Gene Exchange *newsletter.*

United States Public Interest Research Group (U.S. PIRG)
215 Pennsylvania Avenue, S.E.
Washington, DC 20003
The national lobbying office for state PIRGs; student-run organiza-

tions working on environmental protection, consumer protection, and government reform.

World Resources Institute
1709 New York Avenue, N.W., 7th Floor
Washington, DC 20036
Works to provide accurate information about global resources and environmental conditions, analyze emerging issues, and develop creative and workable policy responses.

World Wildlife Fund
1250 24th Street, N.W.
Washington, DC 20037
Provides information on the protection of endangered wildlife, wetlands, and rainforests. Publishes WWF Focus *newsletter bimonthly.*

Worldwatch Institute
1776 Massachusetts Avenue, N.W.
Washington, DC 20036
Works to alert policy makers and the public about emerging global trends in the management of natural and human resources. Publishes Worldwatch *bimonthly.*

Zero Population Growth
1400 16th Street, N.W., Suite 320
Washington, DC 20036
Provides information on population problems and issues. Publishes The ZPG Reporter *bimonthly.*

Fundraising

Foundation Center
79 Fifth Avenue
New York, NY 10003
(800) 424-9836
Maintains collections (in more than 100 U.S. cities) of information on foundations.

Good-Government Organizations

Americans for Democratic Action
1625 K Street, N.W., Suite 210
Washington, DC 20006
Conducts education and lobbying and supports political candidates in support of issues such as health care, family and medical leave, and civil rights.

Citizen Action
1120 19th Street, N.W., Suite 630
Washington, DC 20036

A national political organization attempting to increase citizen participation and offer alternatives in health care, environmental, and economic issues. Publishes Citizen Action News *quarterly.*

Citizens for Tax Justice (CTJ)
1311 L Street, N.W., Suite 400
Washington, DC 20005
Works to give citizens a voice in the development of tax laws at the local, state, and national levels. Advocates a policy of taxation according to ability to pay.

Common Cause
2030 M Street, N.W.
Washington, DC 20036
A nonpartisan citizen group that works to improve government operations through standards of ethics, civil rights, and campaign finance reform. Publishes Common Cause Magazine *bimonthly.*

Congress Watch
215 Pennsylvania Avenue, S.E.
Washington, DC 20003
The legislative advocacy arm of Public Citizen. Represents the public through lobbying, organizing, research, and publications.

Connecticut Citizen Action Group
45 South Main
West Hartford, CT 06107
Organizes Connecticut citizens, conducts public education, and builds coalitions on a variety of issues.

Council of State Governments
444 North Capitol Street, N.W., Suite 401
Washington, DC 20001
Works with the executive and legislative branches of state governments to provide a forum for information exchange and to supply research and communications services.

Government Accountability Project (GAP)
810 First Street, N.E., Suite 630
Washington, DC 20002
Provides legal information and support to whistle-blowers (employees who report on the illegal, corrupt, or wasteful practices of their employers). Runs EPA Watch to monitor activities of the Environmental Protection Agency. Publishes Bridging the GAP *quarterly.*

League of Women Voters
1730 M Street, N.W.
Washington, DC 20036

*A nonpartisan political group working to improve citizen participation in government through voter registration and public debates.
Publishes* The National Voter *magazine bimonthly.*

OMB Watch
1731 Connecticut Avenue, N.W.
Washington, DC 20009
Monitors the Office of Management and Budget, the largest unit within the Executive Office of the President. Provides citizen education on related legislative and administrative issues. Publishes OMB Watcher *bimonthly.*

United States Public Interest Research Group (U.S. PIRG)
215 Pennsylvania Avenue, S.E.
Washington, DC 20003
The national lobbying office for state PIRGs; student-run organizations working on environmental protection, consumer protection, and government reform. Publishes Citizen Agenda *quarterly.*

Health and Nutrition Organizations

Action on Smoking and Health (ASH)
2013 H Street, N.W.
Washington, DC 20006
Takes legal action for nonsmokers' rights, petitions government agencies to limit smoking and enforce existing rules. Publishes Action on Smoking and Health Review *eight times a year.*

Center for Science in the Public Interest (CSPI)
1875 Connecticut Avenue, N.W., Suite 300
Washington, DC 20009
Researches, educates, and advocates on nutrition, diet, food safety, alcohol, and related health issues. Publishes Nutrition Action Healthletter *ten times a year.*

Center for Study of Responsive Law
P.O. Box 19367
Washington, DC 20036
Publishes a variety of consumer-related materials.

Community Nutrition Institute
2001 S Street, N.W., Suite 530
Washington, DC 20009
Works as a public advocate for safe food and health policies by reporting on research and policy developments. Publishes Nutrition Week *weekly.*

Public Citizen Health Research Group
2000 P Street, N.W., Suite 700
Washington, DC 20036

Works to protect the public's health by monitoring the work of the medical establishment, the drug industry, and health-related regulatory agencies. Publishes Health Letter *monthly.*

Public Voice for Food and Health Policy
1001 Connecticut Avenue, N.W., Suite 522
Washington, DC 20036
Works to increase citizen input on food and health issues including federal fish inspection, stronger pesticide regulation, and women's health issues. Publishes Action Alert *quarterly and* Advocacy Update *monthly.*

Human Rights Organizations

Amnesty International USA
322 Eighth Avenue
New York, NY 10001
An independent worldwide movement working for the release of all prisoners of conscience, fair and prompt trials for political prisoners, and an end to torture and executions. Publishes Amnesty Action *bimonthly and* Student Action *monthly for high school and college students.*

Center for Constitutional Rights
666 Broadway, 7th floor
New York, NY 10012
A national public interest law firm working for constitutional and human rights under domestic and international human rights laws. Publishes Annual Docket Report *newsletter twice a year.*

Cultural Survival
215 First Street
Cambridge, MA 02142
Advocates for the rights of indigenous peoples around the globe and works to protect those people from government and corporate oppression. Publishes Cultural Survival Quarterly.

Hunger, Poverty, and Agriculture Organizations

Bread for the World
1100 Wayne Avenue, Suite 1000
Silver Spring, MD 20910
A nationwide Christian movement that lobbies the nation's decision makers, seeking solutions to world hunger. Publishes Current Bread for the World Newsletter *ten times a year.*

Coalition for the Homeless
1234 Massachusetts Avenue, Suite C 1015
Washington, DC 20005

*Operates temporary homes and shelters to help the homeless regain
self-sufficiency and return to independent living.*

Community for Creative Nonviolence (CCNV)
425 Second Street, N.W.
Washington, DC 20001
*Provides direct services to homeless people and works to change U.S.
homeless policy.*

Farm Aid
334 Broadway, Suite 5
Cambridge, MA 02139
*Raises funds and awareness about the loss of family farmers in the
United States; educates on the economic and environmental
impact of the loss of family farmers and the growth of
agribusiness. Publishes* Farm Aid News Weekly *and* Farm Aid
Update *quarterly.*

Food Research and Action Center (FRAC)
1875 Connecticut Avenue, N.W., Suite 540
Washington, DC 20009
*A legal, research, and advocacy center working to end hunger and
malnutrition in the United States. Publishes* Foodlines: A
Chronicle of Hunger and Poverty in America *bimonthly.*

Habitat for Humanity
121 Habitat Street
Americus, Georgia 31709
*Works to end poverty and housing shortages worldwide, largely
through volunteer labor. Publishes* Habitat World *bimonthly.*

Housing Now
425 Second Street, N.W.
Washington, DC 20001
*A coalition of more than one hundred national and local groups
working for affordable housing in the United States.*

Institute for Food and Development Policy/Food First
398 60th Street
Oakland, CA 94618
*Works to educate citizens on the root causes of and solutions to
hunger and poverty. Publishes* Food First News *and* Action
Alert *quarterly.*

National Coalition for the Homeless
1621 K Street, N.W., Suite 1004
Washington, DC 20006
*A federation of individuals, agencies and organizations working to
secure rights, services, and housing for the homeless. Publishes*
Safety Network *monthly.*

National Family Farm Coalition
110 Maryland Avenue, N.E., Suite 205
Washington, DC 20002
Works for progressive agriculture policy reforms to strengthen family farm-based sustainable agriculture.

National Student Campaign Against Hunger and Homelessness
29 Temple Place, 5th floor
Boston, MA 02111
Puts student concerns into action by providing immediate relief to the hungry and homeless with long-term solutions. Publishes Students Making a Difference *quarterly.*

Oxfam America
26 West Street
Boston, MA 02111
Helps fund locally generated grassroots development work in thirty-two countries. Publishes Legislative Alert *newsletter.*

Labor Organizations

American Federation of Labor and Congress of Industrial Organizations (AFL-CIO)
815 16th Street, N.W.
Washington, DC 20006
A national federation of unions that works to promote and foster union organizing campaigns and worker rights.

Coalition of Labor Union Women (CLUW)
1126 16th Street, N.W.
Washington, DC 20036
Works to promote women's issues in the labor movement and increase the number of women in union leadership. Publishes CLUW News *bimonthly.*

Labor Party Advocates
P.O. Box 53177
Washington, DC 20009
Advocates a worker-oriented political agenda and mobilizes support for a labor party. Publishes Labor Party Advocate *bimonthly.*

Midwest Center for Labor Research
3411 West Diversey Street, Room 10
Chicago, IL 60647
A nonprofit consulting group offering economic development services and specializing in maintaining industrial employment. Publishes Early Warning Manual *quarterly and* Labor Research Review.

Mujer Obrera
1113 East Yardell Street
El Paso, TX 79902

Takes direct action against the sweatshop conditions in the sewing industry on the U.S.-Mexico border.

National Safe Workplace Institute
122 South Michigan Avenue, Suite 1450
Chicago, IL 60603
Examines government and corporate policies and programs to advance safety and health in the workplace.

New Directions
P.O. Box 6876
St. Louis, MO 63144
Works for internal democracy and accountability to the membership of the United Auto Workers.

9 to 5, National Association of Working Women
614 Superior Avenue, N.W.
Cleveland, OH 44113
Works to win better pay, rights, and respect on the job for women through organizing, advocacy, and public education. Publishes 9 to 5 Newsletter ten times a year.

Teamsters for a Democratic Union
P.O. Box 10128
Detroit, MI 48210
Works to bring greater internal democracy to the Teamsters Union. Publishes Convoy Dispatch *newspaper.*

United Farm Workers
P.O. Box 62
Keene, CA 93531
Works to end the exploitation of farm workers, promote the availability of safe and affordable food, ban the use of dangerous pesticides, and challenge the strong influence of agribusiness in state and national government.

Media, Communications, and Information Organizations

Center for Investigative Reporting
530 Howard Street, 2nd floor
San Francisco, CA 94105
Works to train journalists in investigative reporting, serves as a base for investigative journalists, and helps educate the public.

Center for the Study of Commercialism
1875 Connecticut Avenue, N.W., Suite 300
Washington, DC 20009
Researches, publicizes, and opposes the invasion of commercial interests in all aspects of society.

69

Children's Express
30 Cooper Square, 4th Floor
New York, NY 10003
*A news service covering children's issues, reported by children and
edited by teenagers.*

Fairness and Accuracy in Reporting (FAIR)
130 West 25th Street
New York, NY 10001
*A national media watch group focusing on the narrow corporate
ownership of the press and its insensitivity to women, labor, and
minorities. Publishes* Extra! *eight times a year.*

Institute for Global Communications/PEACENET/ECONET/
LABORNET
18 De Boom Street
San Francisco, CA 94107
*Operates ECONet and PeaceNet, electronic communications networks
for organizations and individuals involved in environmental,
disarmament, social justice, and peace issues. Publishes*
PeaceNet, World News *and* NetNews *bimonthly.*

Media Access Project
2000 M Street, N.W., Suite 400
Washington, DC 20036
*A public interest law firm working to protect access to information for
the listening and viewing public.*

Media Watch
P.O. Box 618
Santa Cruz, CA 95061
Publishes Media Watch, *a quarterly newsletter dedicated to improv-
ing the image of women in the media.*

Telecommunications Research and Action Center (TRAC)
P.O. Box 12038
Washington, DC 20005
*Represents consumer interests in telecommunications, cable, and
telephone regulatory reform.*

UNPLUG
360 Grand Avenue, Box 385
Oakland, CA 94610
*National youth organization working for commercial free education.
Organizes students to work with parents and teachers for educa-
tional justice.*

American Friends Service Committee (AFSC)
1501 Cherry Street
Philadelphia, PA 19102
*Carries out programs of service, development, justice, and peace to
bring about social improvement. Publishes* Quaker Service
Bulletin *newsletter.*

Center for Defense Information
1500 Massachusetts Avenue, N.W.
Washington, DC 20005
*Opposes excessive expenditures for weapons and policies that increase
the danger of nuclear war by advocating that strong social,
economic, political and military components contribute equally to
the nation's security. Publishes* Defense Monitor *ten times a
year.*

Committee in Solidarity with the People of El Salvador (CISPES)
P.O. Box 12156
Washington, DC 20005
*Works to end U.S. intervention in El Salvador and Central America.
Publishes* Alert! *newspaper monthly.*

Conscience and Military Tax Campaign
4534½ University Way, N.E., Suite 204
Seattle, WA 98105
*Organizes public events and offers counseling and workshops on how
to resist paying taxes used for military purposes. Publishes*
Conscience *quarterly.*

Consortium on Peace Research, Education, and Development
(COPRED)
Center of Conflict Resolution
George Mason University
4400 University Drive
Fairfax, VA 22030
Publishes materials on peace and peace education.

Educators for Social Responsibility
23 Garden Street
Cambridge, MA 02138
*Comprised of teachers, administrators, parents, and other concerned
citizens working to implement conflict resolution and negotiation
in the schools. Publishes* Forum *twice a year.*

Fellowship of Reconciliation (FOR)
523 North Broadway, P.O. Box 271
Nyack, NY 10960

Works on peace and human rights issues focusing on racial and economic justice, nonviolent resolution, and global disarmament. Publishes Fellowship *eight times a year.*

National Campaign for a Peace Tax Fund
2121 Decatur Place, N.W.
Washington, DC 20008
Works for legislation that would allow persons opposed to war to have the military portion of their taxes go into a trust fund for projects that enhance peace.

National Peace Institute Foundation
1835 K Street, N.W.
Washington, DC 20006
A nongovernmental group concerned with the development of the U.S. Institute of Peace, peace education, conflict resolution, the United Nations, and the Alliance for Our Common Future. Publishes Peace Reporter *quarterly.*

Neighbor to Neighbor (N2N)
2601 Mission Street, Room 400
San Francisco, CA 94110
A national grassroots organization working to end U.S. intervention in Central America, for a foreign policy based on democratic ideals, and for health care reform.

Peace Action
1819 H Street, N.W., Suite 640
Washington, DC 20006
A grassroots national organization working to educate, recruit members and organize a citizen's movement with the sustained political power to abolish nuclear weapons, end the international arms trade, and redirect federal spending from the Pentagon to meet human needs. Publishes Peace Action *newsletter quarterly.*

Peace Education Resource Center
2437 North Grant Boulevard
Milwaukee, WI 53210
Publishes curriculum materials on peace issues for schools, churches, synagogues, and communities.

Physicians for Social Responsibility
1101 14th Street, N.W., Suite 700
Washington, DC 20005
A nationwide organization of physicians and others whose main goal is nuclear disarmament. The organization also works on shifting federal budget priorities away from military spending and toward spending on basic human needs such as housing, education, and health care and on environmental effects on health, such as the effects of toxic pollution.

Union of Concerned Scientists
26 Church Street
Cambridge, MA 02238
An organization of scientists concerned about the impact of advanced technology on society, including peace issues. Publishes Nucleus *magazine quarterly and* The Gene Exchange *newsletter.*

War Resisters League
339 Lafayette Street
New York, NY 10012
Helps provide educational information on peace and war resistance through a variety of publications. Publishes The Nonviolent Activist *eight times a year.*

Women's Action for Nuclear Disarmament (WAND)
P.O. Box B
Arlington, MA 02174
Works to increase women's political power and to eliminate weapons of mass destruction and redirect military resources to human and environmental needs. Publishes WAND Bulletin *and* WAND Activists.

Women's International League for Peace and Freedom
1213 Race Street
Philadelphia, PA 19107
Works to achieve social, political, economic, and psychological conditions to ensure peace and freedom throughout the world. Publishes Peace and Freedom *six times a year.*

World Federalist Association
418 Seventh Street, S.E.
Washington, DC 20003
Attempts to abolish war and preserve a livable world through a just and enforceable World Law.

Speakers' Bureaus

Committee on Common Security
Institute for Peace and International Security
91 Harvey Street
Cambridge, MA 02140
Members include Bella Abzug, Richard Barnet and Marcus Raskin of the Institute for Policy Studies, Gloria Steinem, Joseph Lowery of the Southern Christian Leadership Conference, Alice Tepper Marlin of the Council on Economic Priorities, and Victor Navasky of The Nation.

K & S Speakers
875 Main Street
Cambridge, MA 02139

Speakers include Dr. Helen Caldicott, founding president of Physicians for Social Responsibility and founder of Women's Action for Nuclear Disarmament; Seymour Hersh, Pulitzer Prize-winning investigative journalist; Noam Chomsky; and Howard Zinn, historian and author of A People's History of the United States.

Jodi F. Solomon Speakers' Bureau
281 Huntington Avenue, Suite 112
Boston, MA 02115
Provides speakers on cultural awareness, economics, education, the environment, current issues, political issues, social focus, journalism, and more.

Speak Out!
South End Press
116 St. Botolph Street
Boston, MA 02115
A political speakers' bureau that includes U.S. foreign policy critics Noam Chomsky and Edward Herman, Native American activists Ward Churchill and Winona La Duke, peace organizers Daniel Ellsberg and Leslie Cagan, African-American activist Stokely Carmichael, labor leaders, writers, poets, citizen organizers, professors, economists, and environmentalists.

Student, University, and Youth Service Organizations

Amnesty International
National Student Program
1118 22nd Street, N.W.
Washington, DC 20037
The 2,200 campus-based chapters are part of an independent worldwide movement working for the release of all prisoners of conscience, fair and prompt trials for political prisoners, and an end to torture and executions.

Campus Outreach Opportunity League (COOL)
411 Washington Avenue
St. Paul, MN 55108
Facilitates student involvement in community problem-solving efforts, provides organizing resources and training, and publishes a newsletter.

Cool It!
National Wildlife Federation
1400 16th Street, N.W.
Washington, DC 20036
Launched by the National Wildlife Federation to challenge college students to begin solving the problem of global environmental

degradation. *Official "Cool It!" projects are active on more than two hundred college campuses. Publishes* Cool It! Connection *newsletter.*

National Association of Partners in Education (NAPE)
209 Madison Street, Suite 401
Alexandria, VA 22314
Develops collaborative efforts between schools and community organizations and businesses to improve the academic and personal growth of young people.

National Association of Secondary School Principals
1904 Association Drive
Reston, VA 22091
Publishes The Student Council Advisor *and formed the American Student Council Association to help schools establish student councils.*

National Student Campaign Against Hunger and Homelessness
29 Temple Place, 5th floor
Boston, MA 02111
Puts student concerns into action by providing immediate relief to the hungry and homeless and long-term solutions. Publishes Students Making a Difference *quarterly.*

New York Public Interest Research Group (NYPIRG)
9 Murray Street
New York, NY 10007
A student-run statewide environmental and consumer organization working on solid-waste issues, nuclear power, and incineration.

Public Allies
815 15th Street, N.W., Suite 610
Washington, DC 20005
Conducts yearlong workshops that inspire and develop new leaders. Places young people between the ages of 18 and 30 in public sector apprenticeships. Provides training and support in public life.

Public Interest Research Groups
National Campus Program Office
29 Temple Place
Boston, MA 02111

Student Pug-Wash, USA
1638 R Street, N.W., Room 32
Washington, DC 20009
Student-run groups active on 120 college campuses, educate young people on the relevance of science and technology to their lives and on its ability to shape the future of global activity through

interdisciplinary activities focusing on leadership, development, and interactive learning. Publishes Tough Questions *newsletter quarterly.*

United States Public Interest Research Group (U.S. PIRG)
215 Pennsylvania Avenue, S.E.
Washington, DC 20003
The national lobbying office for student-run state PIRGs. Focuses on environmental and consumer protection and energy and government reform. Publishes Citizen Agenda *quarterly.*

United States Student Association (USSA)
815 15th Street, N.W., Suite 838
Washington, DC 20005
Works for student empowerment by lobbying Congress and training students around the country in direct action organizing. Publishes Legislative Update *biweekly when Congress is in session.*

UNPLUG
360 Grand Avenue, Box 385
Oakland, CA 94610
National youth organization working for commercial free education. Organizes students to work with parents and teachers for educational justice.

Youth Action
1830 Connecticut Avenue, N.W.
Washington, DC 20009
Works with young people ages 14 to 25, encouraging them to address social, economic, and environmental issues that affect them and their communities. Publishes The Noise! *quarterly.*

Youth Service America
1101 15th Street, N.W., Suite 200
Washington, DC 20005
Runs the Youth Volunteer Corps of America, which involves students aged 12 to 18 in intensive team service projects sponsored and managed by local nonprofit and community service organizations.

U.S. Government Agencies

Consumer Product Safety Commission (CPSC)
5401 Westbard Avenue
Bethesda, MD 20207
Responsible for protecting the public against "unreasonable" risks of injury associated with consumer products, assisting consumers in evaluating the safety of consumer products, developing uniform safety standards for consumer products, and promoting research and investigation into causes and prevention of product-related injuries.

Department of Agriculture (USDA)
14th Street and Independence Avenue, S.W.
Washington, DC 20250
Responsible for encouraging proper management and conservation of U.S. natural resources, management of the National Forest System, rural development, and protecting consumers by inspecting the meat and poultry industry.

Department of Commerce
Bureau of the Census
Washington, DC 20233
Conducts the national census to determine congressional representation. Also generates data to aid in government decisions regarding demographics and economic policy.

Department of Education
400 Maryland Avenue, S.W.
Washington, DC 20202
Responsible for ensuring access to equal educational opportunity, assisting state and local school systems, and promoting educational improvements.

Department of Health and Human Services (HHS)
200 Independence Avenue, S.W.
Washington, DC 20585
Responsible for administering U.S. welfare and Social Security programs, Medicare and Medicaid programs, and other human service and health programs.

Department of Labor
200 Constitution Avenue, N.W.
Washington, DC 20210
Responsible for fostering, promoting, and developing the welfare of U.S. wage earners. Also responsible for improving working conditions and opportunities for profitable employment. Administers federal labor laws guaranteeing workers' rights.

Environmental Protection Agency (EPA)
401 M Street, S.W.
Washington, DC 20460
Responsible for enforcement of federal environmental law. Publishes EPA Journal bimonthly.

Federal Communications Commission (FCC)
Consumer Assistance Division
1919 M Street, N.W., Room 254
Washington, DC 20554
Charged with regulating interstate and international communications by radio, television, wire, satellite, and cable.

Federal Election Commission (FEC)
999 E Street, N.W.
Washington, DC 20463
Responsible for federal election record keeping.

Federal Information Center
P.O. Box 600
Cumberland, MD 21502
Answers questions about how the federal government works.

Federal Trade Commission (FTC)
Bureau of Consumer Protection
Office of Consumer/Business Education
Washington, DC 20580
*Responsible for regulation of interstate commerce and protecting the
    public from false and deceptive advertising. Publishes materials
    on a number of consumer issues, including shopping by mail or
    phone, warranties, telemarketing, and health care.*

Food and Drug Administration (FDA)
5600 Fishers Lane, Room 1471
Rockville, MD 20857
*Responsible for protecting citizens from hazardous foods, drugs, and
    cosmetics.*

General Accounting Office (GAO)
441 G Street, N.W.
Washington, DC 20548
*Charged with helping Congress in its oversight of federal programs.
    Reviews federal programs and operations and makes recommenda-
    tions to Congress and agency officials to improve operations and
    make programs more efficient. To request reports or receive
    monthly listings of reports, write to P.O. Box 6015, Gaithersburg,
    MD 20077.*

National Institutes of Health (NIH)
9000 Rockville Pike, Room 344
Bethesda, MD 20892
*Responsible for supporting and conducting biomedical research,
    disseminating information to health professionals and the public,
    and supporting research training.*

National Library of Medicine
U.S. Department of Health and Human Services
TRI Representative
8600 Rockville Pike
Bethesda, MD 20894
*Manages the TOXNET system, which includes the Toxic Release
    Inventory database.*

Nuclear Regulatory Commission (NRC)
1717 H Street, N.W.
Washington, DC 20555
Responsible for licensing and inspecting nuclear facilities and investigating cases involving exposure of workers to unsafe working conditions.

Occupational Safety and Health Administration (OSHA)
United States Department of Labor, N3647
200 Constitution Avenue, N.W.
Washington, DC 20210
Charged with regulating safety and health in the workplace.

Securities and Exchange Commission (SEC)
450 Fifth Street, N.W.
Washington, DC 20549
Charged with regulating public companies, investment companies, and other businesses to protect investors. Regulates business operations and requires filing of disclosure statements.

Video

KIDSNET
6856 Eastern Avenue, N.W., Suite 208
Washington, DC 20012
An electronic database clearinghouse that provides in-depth information, including more than 20,000 educational video and audio sources and current public, commercial and cable television programming for children. The database can be searched by grade level, subject area, or special needs. For those without a computer and modem, the service can be used via telephone.

Franco, Debra. *Alternative Visions: Distributing Independent Media in a Home Video World.* This book discusses the problems of independent video distribution by looking at case studies. Available from Foundation for Independent Video and Film, 625 Broadway, New York, NY 10012; $12.95.

Video and Film Producers and Distributors

American Social History Project
Hunter College
695 Park Avenue, Room 340 North
New York, NY 10021
Produced and distributes the Who Built America? *series, seven half-hour videos that present a social history of the United States from the American Revolution to the Civil War. Accompanied by viewer guides and teacher handbook.*

Asian Cinevision
32 East Broadway
New York, NY 10002
The Asian American Media Reference Guide. *Directory of more than 500 Asian American audiovisual programs.*

Bullfrog Films
P.O. Box 149
Oley, PA 19547
Distributes film and video on environmental issues.

California Newsreel
149 Ninth Street, Room 420
San Francisco, CA 94103
Provides educators, business and community organizations with educational films and videos.

Cambridge Documentary Films, Inc.
242 Lexington Avenue
Cambridge, MA 02138
Eugene Debs and the American Movement. *A biographical documentary of working people during the turbulent rise of capitalism in the United States.*

Still Killing Us Softly: Advertising's Image of Women. *Thirty-minute film about advertising's continuing assault on the self-images of women, men, and children.*

Center for Defense Information
1500 Massachusetts Avenue, N.W.
Washington, DC 20005
America's Defense Monitor. *Half-hour video tapes with discussion guides and up-to-date suggestions for further reading; $25.*

Churchill Films
12210 Nebraska Avenue
Los Angeles, CA 90025
Distributes more than four hundred videos and films for young people, with a special emphasis on health issues.

Cinema Guild
1697 Broadway, Suite 506
New York, NY 10019
Distributes over four hundred social documentaries.

Direct Cinema Limited
P.O. Box 10003
Santa Monica, CA 90410
Distributes 350 social documentaries.

Educational Film and Video Project
5332 College Avenue, Suite 101
Oakland, CA 94618
*Produces and distributes film and video about the nuclear arms race,
U.S. policy in Central America, and the global environment.*

Educational Video Center
60 East 13th Street
New York, NY 10003
*Teaches inner-city youth to produce video documentaries on relevant
issues.*

Empowerment Project
3403 Highway 54 West
Chapel Hill, NC 27516
Produced and distributes Coverup: Behind the Iran-Contra Affair
and The Panama Deception, *winner of the 1992 Academy
Award for best documentary.*

Filmmakers Library
124 East 40th Street, Suite 901
New York, NY 11016
Distributes independent film and video to educators.

Films Incorporated
5547 North Ravenswood Avenue
Chicago, IL 60640
Alice Walker. *Profiles the author of the Pulitzer Prize-winning novel*
The Color Purple, *tracing Walker's deep sense of personal
mission and strong sense of self that helped her triumph over her
humble beginnings as the eighth child of a Georgia sharecropper.*
Gloria Steinem. *Profiles a leader of the women's rights movement
and founder of* Ms. *magazine.*

First Run/Icarus Films
200 Park Avenue South, Suite 1319
New York, NY 10003
Born in Flames. *A futuristic tale of feminist turmoil that is still
brewing years after a "peaceful" social revolution.*
Bread and Roses Too. *A film that underscores the role labor unions
can play in the lives of working men and women.*
Fundi: The Story of Ella Baker. *A highlight of the turbulent years
of the 1960s.*
I Am Somebody. *When four hundred poorly paid black women hospital
workers in Charleston, South Carolina, went on strike in 1969 to
demand union recognition and an increase in their hourly wage, they
soon found that they were confronting not only their employers but
also the National Guard and the power of the state government.*

The War at Home. *Highlights the Vietnam struggle on the home front with interviews of students, community leaders, and veterans.*

Greenpeace
1436 U Street, N.W.
Washington, DC 20009
Before It's Too Late. *Highlights six communities around the country fighting to shut down or prevent the construction of facilities that produce toxic waste; $19.95.*
Greenpeace's Greatest Hits. *A sixty-minute film that portrays Greenpeace's major campaigns from 1971 to 1988; $29.95.*

Highlander Research and Education Center
Route 3, Box 370
New Market, TN 37820
You Got to Move. *A documentary about personal and social transformation. Shows how Tennessee's legendary Highlander Folk School and other individuals worked for civil, environmental, and women's rights in the South.*

INFACT
256 Hanover Street, 3rd floor
Boston, MA 02113
Deadly Deception: General Electric, Nuclear Weapons, and Our Environment. *A half-hour Academy Award–winning video.*

Intermedia
1600 Dexter Avenue, North
Seattle, WA 98109
Distributes educational film and video for young people.

Media Network
39 West 14th Street, Suite 403
New York, NY 10011
Images of Color. *Catalog of more than eighty films, video tapes and slide shows on issues affecting Asian, African, Latino, and Native American communities; $11.50 for institutions and organizations, $6.50 for individuals.*
In Her Own Image: Films and Videos Empowering Women for the Future. *Catalog of over eighty films and videos by and about women; $11.50.*
Safe Planet: The Guide to Environmental Film and Video. *Evaluates more than eighty films and videos for use by educators and others. The topics include hazardous waste, recycling, global warming, and workplace hazards; $11.50 for institutions. $7.50 for individuals.*
Seeing Through AIDS. *Catalog of more than eighty titles addressing AIDS and related issues, including women and AIDS, and youth AIDS activism; $11.50 for institutions. $6.50 for individuals.*

Museum of the American Indian
Film and Video Center
3753 Broadway at 155th Street
New York, NY 10032
Native Americans on Film and Video. *Catalog of works by and
about Native Americans.*

National Organization for Women (NOW)
1000 16th Street, N.W., Suite 700
Washington, DC 20036
We Won't Go Back! *Documents the April 1992 March for Women's
Lives in Washington, D.C. and the struggle to protect abortion
rights and reproductive freedom in the United States.*

New Day Films
121 West 27th Street
New York, NY 10001
Union Maids.

People for the American Way
1850 M Street, N.W., Suite 700
Washington, DC 20036
Censorship in Our Schools: Hawkins County, TN. *A video about
a schoolhouse in a small rural community that became a censorship battleground when religious fundamentalists move to ban an
established reading series; $20.*

Third World Newsreel
335 West 38th Street, 5th floor
New York, NY 10018
Produces and distributes video on international and domestic social issues.

Warner Home Video
4000 Warner Boulevard
Burbank, CA 91522
Roger and Me. *Written and directed by Michael Moore. A
docucomedy of what happened to the community of Flint, Michigan (home of the Flint sit-down strike) during the 1980s as
General Motors closed auto factories, laid off workers, and moved
its jobs overseas.*

William Greaves Productions, Inc.
230 West 55th Street, Room 26D
New York, NY 10019
Ida B. Wells: A Passion for Justice.

Women Make Movies
462 Broadway, Suite 500
New York, NY 10013
Produces and distributes film and video by and about women.

Center for Women Policy Studies
2000 P Street, N.W., Suite 508
Washington, DC 20036
*Conducts policy, research, development, and advocacy programs
concentrating on educational equity, work and family issues, and
reproductive rights and health.*

Fund for the Feminist Majority
1600 Wilson Boulevard, Suite 704
Arlington, VA 22209
*Works to eliminate sex discrimination and to promote equality,
reproductive rights, and a feminist agenda through research,
lobbying, litigation, direct action, and public education. Publishes*
Feminist Majority Report *bimonthly.*

Institute for Women's Policy Research
1400 20th Street, N.W., Suite 104
Washington, DC 20036
*Conducts feminist-oriented research for policy makers, legislators, and
women's advocacy organizations.*

National Abortion Rights Action League
1156 15th Street, N.W., Suite 700
Washington, DC 20005
*Works to guarantee every woman the right to choose and obtain a
legal abortion. Publishes* Campus Newsletter *quarterly.*

National Asian Women's Health Organization
440 Grand Avenue, Suite 208
Oakland, CA 94610
*Addresses the health needs of a diverse population of Asian women
through community education, referrals, empowerment, and
policy development and advocacy.*

National Black Women's Health Project
1237 Ralph D. Abernathy Boulevard, S.W.
Atlanta, GA 30310
*Works to define, promote, and maintain the physical, mental, and
emotional well-being of black women.*

National Clearinghouse on Marital and Date Rape
2325 Oak Street
Berkeley, CA 94708
*Provides current information on legislation, litigation, and attitudes
condoning the targeting of women and children for abuse.*

National Coalition Against Domestic Violence
1511 K Street, N.W., Suite 409
Washington, DC 20005

*A national group of grassroots shelter and service programs for
battered women providing technical assistance and training to end
personal and societal violence against women and children.
Publishes* The Voice *three times a year.*

National Congress of Neighborhood Women
249 Manhattan Avenue
Brooklyn, NY 11211
*Works to strengthen women's leadership roles in neighborhoods by
giving support, information, training, and recognition for their
work.*

National Latina Women's Health Organization
P.O. Box 7567
Oakland, CA 94601
*Works to promote Latina health and reproductive rights through
education, advocacy, self-empowerment, outreach, and research.*

National Organization for Women (NOW)
1000 16th Street, N.W. Suite 700
Washington, DC 20036
*Works for legal, political, social, and economic change to bring
women into participation in the mainstream of American
society.*

National Woman's Party
144 Constitution Avenue, N.E.
Washington, DC 20002
*Works for passage of the Equal Rights Amendment to the U.S.
Constitution.*

National Women's Health Network
1325 G Street, N.W.
Washington, DC 20005
*Advocates for better health policies for women and provides informa-
tion to individual women to enable them to have more control
over health decisions.*

National Women's History Project
7738 Bell Road
Windsor, CA 95492
Publishes books, videos, and classroom materials on women's history.

National Women's Political Caucus
1275 K Street, N.W., Suite 750
Washington, DC 20005
*Works to elect and appoint women to public office while promoting
economic freedom, reproductive freedom, and equal rights for
women. Publishes* Women's Political Times *quarterly.*

Older Women's League (OWL)
666 11th Street, N.W., Suite 700
Washington, DC 20001
*A grassroots group working on health-care, employment, care-giving,
pension, and other issues affecting women in midlife and after.
Publishes* OWL Observer *bimonthly.*

Planned Parenthood Federation of America, Inc.
810 Seventh Avenue
New York, NY 10019
*Works for reproductive health services and education dedicated to each
individual's right to an independent decision about having
children.*

Wider Opportunities for Women (WOW)
1325 G Street, N.W., Lower Level
Washington, DC 20005
*Works with economically disadvantaged women to help them achieve
economic independence and equality. Publishes* Women at Work
twice a year.

Women's Legal Defense Fund (WLDF)
1875 Connecticut Avenue, N.W., Suite 710
Washington, DC 20009
*Conducts lobbying, litigation, and community organizing to achieve
equality for women by working on issues including family and
medical leave, affirmative action, sexual harassment, and wage
discrimination. Publishes* WLDF News *twice a year.*

NOTES

1. Ralph Nader and Donald Ross, *Action for a Change: A Student's Manual for Public Interest Organizing.* rev. ed. (New York: Grossman, 1972), 3.

2. Jon Naar, *Design for a Livable Planet: How You Can Help Clean Up the Environment* (New York: HarperCollins, 1990), 274, 275.

3. Charles L. Smith, *The Hobby of Pamphleteering* (Berkeley, Calif.: Charles L. Smith, 1962; rev., 1989).

4. Don Engdahl, "Pamphleteer Stalks Bodega Bay A-Plant," *Santa Rosa Press Democrat,* Sept. 5, 1963, p. 22.

5. Smith, Hobby of Pamphleteering.

6. David Bollier, *Citizen Action and Other Big Ideas: A History of Ralph Nader and the Modern Consumer Movement* (Washington, D.C.: Center for Study of Responsive Law, 1989), 39–40.

7. "The Struggle for Worker Safety," *Bridging the GAP,* Fall 1991, 1–2.

8. Ibid.

9. Bollier, *Citizen Action,* 40.

10. Mark Green with Michael Waldman, Michael Calabrese, Lynn Darling, Bruce Rosenthal, James M. Fallows, and David R. Zwick, *Who Runs Congress?* 4th ed. (New York: Dell, 1984), 377.

11. Stephen A. Newman and Nancy Kramer, *Getting What You Deserve: A Handbook for the Assertive Consumer* (Garden City, N.Y.: Doubleday, 1979), 293.

12. Marc Caplan, *A Citizens' Guide to Lobbying* (New York: Dembner Books, 1983), 62.

13. Ibid., 63.

14. Ibid., 71.

15. Janet Kelsey and Don Wiener, "The Citizen/Labor Energy Coalition," *Social Policy,* Spring 1983, 16.

16. Lee Staples, ed., *Roots to Power: A Manual for Grassroots Organizing* (New York: Praeger, 1984), 1.

17. Ibid., 4–6.

18. Si Kahn, *Organizing: A Guide for Grassroots Leaders,* rev. ed. (Silver Spring, Md.: National Association of Social Workers, 1991), 10.

19. Kim Bobo, Jackie Kendall, and Steve Max, *Organizing for Social Change: A Manual for Activists in the 1990s* (Washington, D.C.: Seven Locks Press, 1991), 29.

20. Harry C. Boyte, *The Backyard Revolution: Understanding the New Citizen Movement* (Philadelphia: Temple University Press, 1980), 49–50.

21. Ibid., 51.

22. Anne Witte Garland, "Gale Cincotta," *Ms.*, January 1986, 51, 101.

23. Caplan, *Citizens' Guide to Lobbying*, 65.

24. Kahn, *Organizing*, 104, 108–110.

25. Dolores Huerta, "Reflections on the UFW Experience," *Center Magazine*, July-August 1985, 2.

26. Ibid.

27. Ibid., 2–3.

28. Nancy Brigham, Maria Catalfio, and Dick Cluster, *How to Do Leaflets, Newsletters and Newspapers* (Detroit: PEP Publishers, 1991), 9–11.

29. Charles L. Smith, *Uses of a Clearinghouse: Mutual Self-Help in Any Organization* (Berkeley, Calif.: Charles L. Smith, 1989).

30. Brigham et al., *How to Do Leaflets, Newsletters and Newspapers*, 19.

31. United States Public Interest Research Group, "Nuclear Power Industry PACs Gave over $25 Million to Congressional Candidates, 1981–1988; Key Nuclear Licensing Vote Coming Up in House," press release, September 15, 1989, 1, 2.

32. Russell Mokhiber and Leonard Shen, "Love Canal," in *Who's Poisoning America? Corporate Polluters and Their Victims in the Chemical Age*, ed. Ralph Nader, Ronald Brownstein, and John Richard (San Francisco: Sierra Club Books, 1981), 296.

33. League of Women Voters, *Speaking Out: Setting Up a Speakers' Bureau* (Washington, D.C.: League of Women Voters, 1977).

34. Bj King-Taylor, Physicians for Social Responsibility, personal interview, November 1991.

35. Green et al., *Who Runs Congress?* 392.

36. Bobo et al., *Organizing for Social Change, 29, 36.

37. Will Collette, "Research for Organizing," in Staples, *Roots to Power*, 144, 148, 149.

38. Bollier, *Citizen Action*, 37, 44–45.

39. Ibid., 37.

40. OMB Watch, *Using Community Right to Know: A Guide to a New Federal Law* (Washington, D.C.: OMB Watch, 1988).

41. Bollier, *Citizen Action*, 37.

42. National Library of Medicine, U.S. Department of Health and Human Services, TRI Representative, 8600 Rockville Pike, Bethesda, MD 20894.

43. Bollier, *Citizen Action*, 38.

44. John Ullmann, Jan Colbert, and the Investigative Reporters and Editors, Inc., eds., *The Reporter's Handbook: An Investigator's Guide to Documents and Techniques*, 2nd ed. (New York: St. Martin's Press, 1991), 289.

45. Bollier, Citizen Action, 40.

46. Freedom of Information Clearinghouse, *The Freedom of Information Act: A User's Guide* (Washington, D.C.: Freedom of Information Clearinghouse, 1989); Elaine P. English, *How to Use the Federal FOI Act*, 5th ed. (Washington, D.C.: The FOI Service Center, 1985), 3.

47. Bollier, *Citizen Action*, 40–41.

48. Ibid., 39.

49. Athan G. Theoharis, "FBI Surveillance During the Cold War Years: A Constitutional Crisis," *Public Historian*, Winter 1981, 10.

50. Ibid.

51. Leon Friedman, in Letty Cottin Pogrebin, "Have You Ever Supported Equal Pay, Child Care or Women's Groups?: The FBI Was Watching You," *Ms.*, June 1977, 42.

52. John W. Moore, "Old Ghosts, Future Shock," National Journal, December 30, 1989, 3105.

53. Bollier, *Citizen Action*, 43.

54. English, *How to Use the Federal FOI Act*, 3.

55. Ibid., 4.

56. FOI Clearinghouse, *Freedom of Information Act*.

57. English, *How to Use the Federal FOI Act*, 5.

58. Ibid.

59. Ibid., 7.

60. FOI Clearinghouse, *Freedom of Information Act*.

61. Ibid.

62. "Reagan's Inaugural Festivities Win Proxmire's Fleece Award," Reuters wire service, March 31, 1987.

63. Penny Loeb, "Investigating Politicians," in Ullmann et al., *Reporter's Handbook*, 148.

64. Common Cause, *Background Information on Campaign Finance Reform and Honoraria: U.S. Senate*, fact sheet (Washington, D.C.: Common Cause, 1990).

65. Kathleen A. Welch, "Democracy for Sale: The Need for Campaign Finance Reform," *In the Public Interest*, Spring 1990, 35.

66. Loeb, "Investigating Politicians," 149.

67. Staples, *Roots to Power*, 3.

68. Newman and Kramer, *Getting What You Deserve*, 307.

69. Kahn, *Organizing*, 174–175.

70. Paul Angiolillo and Aaron Bernstein, "The Secondary Boycott Gets a Second Wind," *Business Week*, June 27, 1988, 82.

71. Institute for Consumer Responsibility, interview, December 1991.

72. Nancy Gaschott, "Babies at Risk: Infant Formula Still Takes Its Toll," *Multinational Monitor*, October 1986, 11.

73. Russell Mokhiber, "Infant Formula: Hawking Disaster in the Third World," *Multinational Monitor*, April 1987, 20.

74. Gaschott, "Babies at Risk," 12.

75. Mokhiber, Infant Formula, 20.

76. Gaschott, "Babies at Risk," 11.

77. John Summa, "Killing Them Sweetly," *Multinational Monitor*, November 1988, 28.

78. Gaschott, "Babies at Risk," 11.

79. Ibid.

80. "Nestlé: The Boycott's Back," *Multinational Monitor*, September 1988, 4.

81. Newman and Kramer, *Getting What You Deserve*, 306.

82. Ibid., 305–306.

83. Green et al., *Who Runs Congress?* 364.

84. Kahn, *Organizing*, 247.

85. Robert Weissman, "Replacing the Union: Business's Labor Offensive," *Multinational Monitor*, April 1991, 10–12.

86. Kim Moody, *An Injury to All: The Decline of American Unionism* (New York: Verso, 1988), 303; Bureau of Labor Statistics, U.S. Department of Labor, 1992.

87. Holley Knaus, "Labor's Lost Right to Strike," *Multinational Monitor*, July-August 1992, 36.

88. Harvard Sitkoff, *The Struggle for Black Equality: 1954–1980* (New York: Hill and Wang, 1981), pp. 41–58.

89. Ibid., 81.

90. Andrea Ayvazian, "No Payment Enclosed: Why I Resist War Taxes," *Progressive*, April 1989, 19–21.

91. Caplan, *Citizens' Guide to Lobbying*, 33.

92. Ibid., 120.

93. Ibid., 38.

94. Green et al., *Who's Runs Congress?* 372, 373.

95. Caplan, *Citizens' Guide to Lobbying*, 31, 32.

96. Green et al., *Who Runs Congress?* 374.

97. Caplan, *Citizens' Guide to Lobbying*, 32.

98. Ibid., 27.

99. Green et al., *Who Runs Congress?* 382.

100. Caplan, *Citizens' Guide to Lobbying*, 42–43.

101. Ibid., 39.

102. Green et al., *Who Runs Congress?* 383–384.

103. Ibid., 384.

104. Caplan, *Citizens' Guide to Lobbying*, 138.

105. Ibid., 153–166.

106. Ibid., 58.

107. Green et al., *Who Runs Congress?* 387.

108. Ibid., 386.

109. Caplan, *Citizens' Guide to Lobbying*, 175, 176.

110. Green et al., *Who Runs Congress?* 391.

111. Kelley Griffin, *More Action for a Change* (New York: Dembner Books, 1987), 139.

112. Ibid.

113. Ibid., 142, 143.

114. Naar, *Design for a Livable Planet*, 251.

115. Gary Cohen and John O'Connor, *Fighting Toxics: A Manual for Protecting Your Family, Community and Workplace* (Washington, D.C.: Island Press, 1990), 217–220.

116. Naar, *Design for a Livable Planet*, 247.

117. Cohen and O'Connor, *Fighting Toxics*, 221.

118. Naar, *Design for a Livable Planet*, 247.

119. Cohen and O'Connor, *Fighting Toxics*, 212.

120. League of Women Voters Education Fund, *Going to Court in the Public Interest: A Guide for Community Groups* (Washington, D.C.: League of Women Voters, 1983), 3.

121. Newman and Kramer, *Getting What You Deserve*, 275.

122. Ibid., 281.

123. Kenneth Lasson and the Public Citizen Litigation Group, *Representing Yourself: What You Can Do Without a Lawyer* (Washington, D.C.: Public Citizen, 1983), 136.

124. Ibid., 140.

125. Newman and Kramer, *Getting What You Deserve*, 283.

126. Ibid., 284–285.

127. Ibid., 285.

128. David D. Schmidt, "Government by the People: Voters Are Writing New Laws Through Initiative and Referendum," *Public Citizen*, June 1986, 14.

129. Ibid.

130. David D. Schmidt, *Citizen Lawmakers: The Ballot Initiative Revolution* (Philadelphia: Temple University Press, 1989), 196, 192.

131. Ibid., 200.

132. Charlene La Voie, *The Community Lawyer Project* (Winchester, Conn.: Community Lawyer, 1991), 2.

133. Ibid., 4.

134. Ibid., 5, 6.

135. Heidi J. Welsh, "Shareholder Activism," *Multinational Monitor*, December 1988, 9–10.

136. United Shareholders Association, *The Shareholder Proposal Process: A Step-by-Step Guide to Shareholder Activism for Individuals and Institutions* (Washington, D.C.: United Shareholders Association, 1987).

137. "Voice of Conscience: An Interview with Timothy Smith," *Multinational Monitor*, December 1988, 21.

138. Welsh, "Shareholder Activism," 9–10.

139. Ibid., 9.

140. "Voice of Conscience," 21.

141. Welsh, "Shareholder Activism," 11.

142. "The Good, the Bad and the Miscreant," *Multinational Monitor*, December 1988, 5.

143. Ralph Nader and Steven Gold, "Letters to the Editor: How About a Little Down-Home *Glasnost?" Columbia Journalism Review*, September/October 1988, 53.

144. Ibid., 54.

145. Bobo et al., *Organizing for Social Change*, 28.

146. Bollier, *Citizen Action*, 28.

147. Bobo et al., *Organizing for Social Change*, 181.

148. Ibid., 177.

149. Jill R. Shellow and Nancy C. Stella, eds., *Grant Seekers Guide*, 3rd ed. (Mt. Kisco, N.Y.: Moyer Bell, 1989); The Foundation Center, *The Foundation Directory*, 11th ed. (New York: Columbia University Press, 1987); Foundation Center, 79 Fifth Avenue, New York, NY 10003; (800) 424-9836.

150. *Non-Profit Organizations, Public Policy and the Political Process: A Guide to the Internal Revenue Code and Federal Election Campaign Act* (Washington, D.C.: Perkins Coie, 1987), 3.

151. Ibid., 23.

152. U.S. Internal Revenue Service, *Tax Exempt Status for Your Organization* (Washington, D.C.: U.S. Internal Revenue Service, 1989).

153. Norman J. Kiritz, "Program Planning and Proposal Writing," in *The Rich Get Richer and the Poor Write Proposals*, ed. Nancy Mitiguy (Amherst: University of Massachusetts Citizen Involvement Training Project, 1978), 43–48, 59.

154. Patricia Read, *Foundation Fundamentals: A Resource Guide for Grantseekers*, 3rd ed. (New York: The Foundation Center, 1986); Michael S. Seltzer, *Securing Your Organization's Future: A Complete Guide to Fundraising Strategies* (New York: The Foundation Center, 1987).

BIBLIOGRAPHY

Books

Alinsky, Saul. *Reveille for Radicals.* New York: Vintage Books, 1969.

Alinsky, Saul. *Rules for Radicals.* New York: Random House, 1971.

American Social History Project, under the direction of Herbert G. Gutman. *Who Built America? Working People and the Nation's Economy, Politics, Culture and Society.* 2 vols. New York: Pantheon, 1989, 1992.

Angiolillo, Paul, and Aaron Bernstein. "The Secondary Boycott Gets a Second Wind," *Business Week,* June 27, 1988.

Ayvazian, Andrea. "No Payment Enclosed: Why I Resist War Taxes," *Progressive,* April 1989.

Bagdikian, Ben H. *The Media Monopoly.* 3rd ed. Boston: Beacon Press, 1990.

Baran, Paul, and Paul Sweezy. *Monopoly Capital: An Essay on the American Economy and Social Order.* New York: Monthly Review Press, 1966.

Barnet, Richard J., and Ronald E. Muller. *Global Reach: The Power of the Multinational Corporations.* New York: Touchstone Books, 1976.

Berkeley Information Network fact sheet. Berkeley, Calif.: Berkeley Public Library, 1991.

Bobo, Kim, Jackie Kendall and Steve Max. *Organizing for Social Change: A Manual for Activists in the 1990s.* Washington, D.C.: Seven Locks Press, 1991.

Bollier, David. *Citizen Action and Other Big Ideas: A History of Ralph Nader and the Modern Consumer Movement.* Washington, D.C.: Center for Study of Responsive Law, 1989.

Bollier, David, and Joan Claybrook. *Freedom from Harm: The Civilizing Influence of Health, Safety and Environmental Regulation.* Washington, D.C.: Public Citizen and Democracy Project, 1986.

Boston Women's Health Book Collective. *The New Our Bodies, Ourselves.* New York: Simon & Schuster, 1992.

Boyer, Richard, and Herbert Morais. *Labor's Untold Story.* New York: United Electrical, Radio and Machine Workers of America, 1986. Originally published 1955.

Boyte, Harry C. *The Backyard Revolution: Understanding the New Citizen Movement.* Philadelphia: Temple University Press, 1980.

Boyte, Harry C. *Community Is Possible*. New York: Harper Collins, 1984.

Braverman, Harry. *Labor and Money Capital: The Degradation of Work in the Twentieth Century*. New York: Monthly Review Press, 1976.

Brigham, Nancy, Maria Catalfio, and Dick Cluster. *How to Do Leaflets, Newsletters and Newspapers*. Detroit: PEP Publishers, 1991.

Brodeur, Paul. *Outrageous Misconduct: The Asbestos Industry on Trial*. New York: Pantheon, 1985.

Brown, Dee Alexander. *Bury My Heart at Wounded Knee*. Austin, Texas: Holt, Rinehart and Winston, 1971.

Buhle, Paul, and Alan Dawley, eds. *Working for Democracy: American Workers from the Revolution to the Present*. Urbana: University of Illinois Press, 1985.

Cahn, Edgar and Jonathan Rowe. *Time Dollars: The New Currency That Enables Americans to Turn Their Hidden Resource—Time—into Personal Security and Community Renewal*. Emmaus, Pa.: Rodale Press, 1992.

Cantarow, Ellen, with Susan Gushee O'Malley and Sharon Hartman Strom. *Moving the Mountain: Women Working for Social Change*. Old Westbury, N.Y.: Feminist Press, 1980.

Caplan, Marc. *A Citizens' Guide to Lobbying*. New York: Dembner Books, 1983.

Carmichael, Stokely, and Charles Hamilton. *Black Power: The Politics of Liberation in America*. New York: Vintage Books, 1967.

Carson, Clayborne. *In Struggle: SNCC and the Black Awakening of the 1960s*. Cambridge, Mass.: Harvard University Press, 1981.

Carson, Rachel. *Silent Spring*. Boston: Houghton Mifflin, 1962.

Chomsky, Noam. *Necessary Illusions: Thought Control in Democratic Societies*. Boston: South End Press, 1989.

Citizen's Clearinghouse for Hazardous Waste. *Using Your Right-To-Know: Dealing With Operating Facilities*. Falls Church, Va.: Citizens' Clearinghouse for Hazardous Waste, 1989.

Clark, Septima Poinsette. *Ready from Within: Septima Clark and the Civil Rights Movement*. Ed. Cynthia Stokes Brown. Navarro, Calif.: Wild Trees Press, 1986.

Claybrook, Joan. *Retreat from Safety: Reagan's Attack on America's Health*. New York: Pantheon, 1984.

Cobble, Dorothy Sue, ed. *Women and Unions: Forging a Partnership*. Ithaca, N.Y.: ILR Press, 1993.

Cohen, Gary, and John O'Connor. *Fighting Toxics: A Manual for Protecting Your Family, Community and Workplace.* Washington, D.C.: Island Press, 1990.

Commoner, Barry. *The Closing Circle.* New York: Knopf, 1971.

Commoner, Barry. *Making Peace with the Planet.* New York: Pantheon, 1990.

Common Cause. *Background Information on Campaign Finance Reform and Honoraria: U.S. Senate.* Fact sheet. Washington, D.C.: Common Cause, 1990.

Cowan, Jessica, ed. *Good Works: A Guide to Careers in Social Change.* New York: Barricade Books, 1991.

Davis, Angela. *Women, Race and Class.* New York: Vintage Books, 1983.

Delgado, Gary. *Organizing the Movement: The Roots and Growth of ACORN.* Philadelphia: Temple University Press, 1986.

Dewart, Janet, ed. *The State of Black America, 1989.* New York: The National Urban League, 1989.

Engdahl, Don. "Pamphleteer Stalks Bodega Bay A-Plant," *Santa Rosa Press Democrat,* September 5, 1963.

English, Elaine P. *How to Use the Federal FOI Act.* 5th ed. Washington, D.C.: FOI Service Center, 1985.

Environmental Protection Agency. *School Recycling Programs: A Handbook for Educators.* Washington, D.C.: Environmental Protection Agency, 1990.

Epstein, Samuel. *The Politics of Cancer.* San Francisco: Sierra Club Books, 1978.

Evans, Sara M. *Born for Liberty: A History of Women in America.* New York: Free Press, 1989.

Evans, Sara M. *Personal Politics: The Roots of Women's Liberation in the Civil Rights Movement and the New Left.* New York: Random House, 1979.

Evans, Sara M. and Harry C. Boyte. *Free Spaces: The Sources of Democratic Change in America.* New York: Harper Collins, 1986.

Faludi, Susan. *Backlash: The Undeclared War against American Women.* New York: Crown, 1991.

Flanagan, Joan. *The Grass Roots Fundraising Book: How to Raise Money in Your Community,* 2nd rev. ed. Chicago: Contemporary Books, 1982.

Flexner, Eleanor. *Century of Struggle: The Woman's Rights Movement in the United States.* Rev. ed. Cambridge, Mass.: Belknap Press, 1975. Originally published 1959).

Forman, James. *The Making of Black Revolutionaries*. Washington, D.C.: Open Hand, 1985.

The Foundation Center. *The Foundation Directory*, 11th ed. New York: Columbia University Press, 1987.

Freedom of Information Clearinghouse. *The Freedom of Information Act: A User's Guide*. Washington, D.C.: Freedom of Information Clearinghouse, 1989.

Freeman, Jo, ed. *Social Movements of the Sixties and Seventies*. White Plains, N.Y.: Longman, 1983.

Friedan, Betty. *The Feminine Mystique*. New York: Laurel Books, 1963.

Friere, Paulo. *Pedagogy of the Oppressed*. New York: Free Press, 1963.

Galbraith, John Kenneth. *The Affluent Society*. Boston: Houghton Mifflin, 1958.

Garland, Anne Witte. "Gale Cincotta," *Ms.*, January 1986.

Garland, Anne Witte. *Women Activists: Challenging the Abuse of Power*. Old Westbury, N.Y.: The Feminist Press, 1988.

Gaschott, Nancy. "Babies at Risk: Infant Formula Still Takes Its Toll," *Multinational Monitor*, October 1986.

Gibbs, Lois Marie. *Love Canal: My Story*. Falls Church, Va.: Citizens' Clearinghouse for Hazardous Wastes.

Giddings, Paula. *When and Where I Enter: The Impact of Black Women on Race and Sex in America*. New York: Morrow, 1984.

"The Good, the Bad and the Miscreant," *Multinational Monitor*, December 1988.

Goodwyn, Lawrence. *Democratic Promise: The Populist Moment in America*. New York: Oxford University Press, 1976.

Goodwyn, Lawrence. *The Populist Moment: A Short History of Agrarian Revolt in America*. New York: Oxford University Press, 1978.

Green, Mark, ed. *The Big Business Reader on Corporate America*. New York: Pilgrim Press, 1983.

Green, Mark, with Michael Waldman, Michael Calabrese, Lynn Darling, Bruce Rosenthal, James M. Fallows, and David R. Zwick. *Who Runs Congress?* 4th edition. New York: Dell, 1984.

Greider, William. *Who Will Tell the People? The Betrayal of American Democracy*. New York: Simon & Schuster, 1992.

Griffin, Kelley. *More Action for a Change*. New York: Dembner Books, 1987.

Haley, Alex. *The Autobiography of Malcolm X.* New York: Grove Press, 1965.

Hampton, Henry, and Steve Fayer. *Voices of Freedom: An Oral History of the Civil Rights Movement from the 1950s through the 1980s.* New York: Bantam Books, 1990.

Harrington, Michael. *The Other America.* Baltimore: Pelican, 1971.

Herman, Edward. *Corporate Control, Corporate Power.* New York: Cambridge University Press, 1981.

Herman, Edward, and Noam Chomsky. *Manufacturing Consent: The Political Economy of the Mass Media.* New York: Pantheon, 1988.

Hertsgaard, Mark. *On Bended Knee: The Press and the Reagan Presidency.* New York: Schocken Books, 1988.

Horwitt, Sanford D. *Let Them Call Me Rebel: Saul Alinsky—His Life and Legacy.* New York: Knopf, 1989.

Huerta, Dolores. "Reflections on the UFW Experience," *Center Magazine,* July-August 1985.

Illich, Ivan. *Deschooling Society.* New York: Harper Collins, 1970.

Jezer, Marty. *The Dark Ages: Life in the United States, 1945-1960.* Boston: South End Press, 1982.

Kahn, Si. *Organizing: A Guide for Grassroots Leaders.* Rev. ed. Silver Spring, Md.: National Association of Social Workers, 1991.

Kelsey, Janet, and Don Wiener. "The Citizen/Labor Energy Coalition," *Social Policy,* Spring 1983.

Kiritz, Norman J. "Program Planning and Proposal Writing." In Nancy Mitiguy, ed. *The Rich Get Richer and the Poor Write Proposals.* Amherst: University of Massachusetts Citizen Involvement Training Project, 1978.

Knaus, Holley. "Labor's Lost Right to Strike," *Multinational Monitor,* July-August 1992.

Kozol, Jonathan. *The Night Is Dark and I Am Far from Home.* Boston: Houghton Mifflin, 1975.

Krebs, A. V. *The Corporate Reapers: The Book of Agribusiness.* Washington, D.C.: Essential Books, 1992.

Lappe, Frances Moore. *Diet for a Small Planet.* San Francisco: Institute for Food and Development Policy, 1991.

Lappe, Frances Moore, and Joseph Collins. *Food First: Beyond the Myth of Scarcity.* New York: Ballantine, 1978.

Lasson, Kenneth, and the Public Citizen Litigation Group. *Representing Yourself: What You Can Do Without a Lawyer.* Washington, D.C.: Public Citizen, 1983.

La Voie, Charlene. *The Community Lawyer Project.* Winchester, Conn.: Community Lawyer, 1991.

League of Women Voters. *Speaking Out: Setting Up a Speaker's Bureau.* Washington, D.C.: League of Women Voters, 1977.

League of Women Voters Education Fund. *Going to Court in the Public Interest: A Guide for Community Groups.* Washington, D.C.: League of Women Voters Education Fund, 1983.

Levy, Jacques E. *Cesar Chavez: Autobiography of La Causa.* New York: Norton, 1975.

Lewis, Barbara A. *The Kid's Guide to Social Action: How to Solve the Social Problems You Choose—and Turn Creative Thinking into Positive Action.* Minneapolis: Free Spirit, 1991.

Lewis, Eleanor J., and Eric Weltman. *Forty Ways to Make Government Purchasing Green.* Washington, D.C.: Center for Study of Responsive Law, 1992.

Lynd, Alice, and Staughton Lynd, eds. *Rank and File: Personal Histories by Working-Class Organizers.* New York: Monthly Review Press, 1988. (Originally published 1973.)

Makinson, Larry. *The Price of Admission: An Illustrated Atlas of Campaign Spending in the 1988 Congressional Elections.* Washington, D.C.: Center for Responsive Politics, 1989.

Mierzwinski, Ed, and Lucinda Sikes. *The Big Book of PIRG Consumer Projects.* Washington, D.C.: United States Public Interest Research Group, 1990.

Mintz, Morton, and Jerry S. Cohen. *Power, Inc.* New York: Bantam Books, 1976.

Mokhiber, Russell. *Corporate Crime and Violence: Big Business Power and the Abuse of the Public Trust.* San Francisco: Sierra Club Books, 1988.

Mokhiber, Russell. "Infant Formula: Hawking Disaster in the Third World," *Multinational Monitor,* April 1987.

Mokhiber, Russell, and Leonard Shen. "Love Canal." In Ralph Nader, Ronald Brownstein and John Richard, eds. *Who's Poisoning America? Corporate Polluters and Their Victims in the Chemical Age.* San Francisco: Sierra Club Books, 1981.

Monk, Catherine. *Ralph Nader's Congress Project Profile Kit.* Washington, D.C.: Center for Study of Responsive Law, 1981.

Moody, Kim. *An Injury to All: The Decline of American Unionism*. New York: Verso, 1988.

Moore, W. John. "Old Ghosts, Future Shock," *National Journal*, December 30, 1989.

Morgan, Robin, ed. *Sisterhood Is Powerful: An Anthology of Writings from the Women's Liberation Movement*. New York: Vintage Books, 1970.

Morris, Aldon D. *The Origins of the Civil Rights Movement: Black Communities Organizing for Change*. New York: Free Press, 1984.

Naar, Jon. *Design for a Livable Planet: How You Can Help Clean Up the Environment*. New York: Harper Collins, 1990.

Nader, Ralph. *Unsafe at Any Speed: The Designed-in Dangers of the American Automobile*. New York: Grossman, 1973.

Nader, Ralph, and Donald Ross. *Action for a Change: A Student's Manual for Public Interest Organizing*. Rev. ed. New York: Grossman, 1972.

Nader, Ralph, and Steven Gold. "Letters to the Editor: How About a Little Down-Home *Glasnost?*" *Columbia Journalism Review*, September-October 1988.

National Student Campaign Against Hunger and Homelessness. *Setting a New Course: Expanding Collegiate Curricula to Incorporate the Study of Hunger and Homelessness*. Boston: National Student Campaign Against Hunger and Homelessness, 1990.

"Nestlé: The Boycott's Back," *Multinational Monitor*, September 1988.

Newman, Stephen A., and Nancy Kramer. *Getting What You Deserve: A Handbook for the Assertive Consumer*. Garden City, N.Y.: Doubleday, 1979.

Non-Profit Organizations, Public Policy, and the Political Process: A Guide to the Internal Revenue Code and Federal Election Campaign Act. Washington, D.C.: Perkins Coie, 1987.

OMB Watch. *Using Community Right to Know: A Guide to a New Federal Law*. Washington, D.C.: OMB Watch, 1988.

Paehlke, Robert C. *Environmentalism and the Future of Progressive Politics*. New Haven, Conn.: Yale University Press, 1989.

Pertschuk, Michael. *Giant Killers*. New York: Norton, 1986.

Pertschuk, Michael. *Revolt against Regulation: The Rise and Pause of the Consumer Movement*. Berkeley: University of California Press, 1982.

Pogrebin, Letty Cottin. "Have You Ever Supported Equal Pay, Child Care or Women's Groups? The FBI Was Watching You," *Ms.*, June 1977.

Powledge, Fred. *Free at Last? The Civil Rights Movement and the People Who Made It*. Boston: Little, Brown, 1991.

Preis, Art. *Labor's Giant Step: Twenty Years of the CIO*. New York: Path Press, 1972. (Originally published 1964.)

Project Public Life. *Making the Rules: A Guidebook for Young People Who Intend to Make a Difference*. Minneapolis: Project Public Life, 1991.

Read, Patricia. *Foundation Fundamentals: A Resource Guide for Grantseekers*, 3rd ed. New York: The Foundation Center, 1986.

"Reagan's Inaugural Festivities Win Proxmire's Fleece Award," Reuters wire service, March 31, 1987.

Schmidt, David D. *Citizen Lawmakers: The Ballot Initiative Revolution*. Philadelphia: Temple University Press, 1989.

Schmidt, David D. "Government by the People: Voters Are Writing New Laws Through Initiative and Referendum," *Public Citizen*, June 1986.

Seltzer, Michael S. *Securing Your Organization's Future: A Complete Guide to Fundraising Strategies*. New York: The Foundation Center, 1987.

Serrin, William. *Homestead: The Tragedy of an American Steel Town*. New York: Times Books, 1992.

Shellow, Jill R., and Nancy C. Stella, eds. *Grant Seekers Guide*. 3rd ed. Mount Kisco, N.Y.: Moyer Bell, 1989.

Simpson, Walter. *Recipe for an Effective Campus Energy Conservation Program*. Cambridge, Mass.: Union of Concerned Scientists, 1991.

Sitkoff, Harvard. *The Struggle for Black Equality, 1954–1980*. New York: Hill & Wang, 1981.

Slayton, Robert. *Back of the Yards: The Making of a Local Democracy*. Chicago: University of Chicago Press, 1986.

Smith, Charles L. *The Hobby of Pamphleteering*. Berkeley, Calif.: Charles L. Smith, 1962; rev., 1989.

Smith, Charles L. *Uses of a Clearinghouse: Mutual Self-help in Any Organization*. Berkeley, Calif.: Charles L. Smith, 1989.

Staples, Lee, ed. *Roots to Power: A Manual for Grassroots Organizing*. New York: Praeger, 1984.

Sterling, Dorothy. *Black Foremothers: Three Lives*. Old Westbury, N.Y.: Feminist Press, 1988.

Stern, Philip M. *The Best Congress Money Can Buy*. New York: Pantheon, 1988.

"The Struggle for Worker Safety," *Bridging the Gap,* Fall 1991.

Summa, John. "Killing Them Sweetly," *Multinational Monitor,* November 1988.

Takaki, Ronald. *Strangers from a Different Shore: A History of Asian Americans.* New York: Viking Penguin, 1989.

Terkel, Studs. *Hard Times.* New York: Pantheon, 1970.

Terkel, Studs. *Race: How Blacks and Whites Think and Feel About the American Obsession.* New York: New Press, 1992.

Theoharis, Athan G. "FBI Surveillance During the Cold War Years: A Constitutional Crisis," *Public Historian,* Winter 1981.

Ullmann, John, and Jan Colbert, eds. *Reporter's Handbook: An Investigator's Guide to Documents and Techniques.* 2nd ed. New York: St. Martin's Press, 1991.

United Shareholders Association. *The Shareholder Proposal Process: A Step-by-Step Guide to Shareholder Activism for Individuals and Institutions.* Washington, D.C.: United Shareholders Association, 1987.

United States Public Interest Research Group. "Nuclear Power Industry PACs Gave over $25 Million to Congressional Candidates, 1981–1988; Key Nuclear Licensing Vote Coming Up in House," press release, September 15, 1989.

"Voice of Conscience: An Interview with Timothy Smith,"

Multinational Monitor, December 1988.

Wasserman, Harvey. *Harvey Wasserman's History of the United States.* New York: Four Walls Eight Windows, 1988.

Weir, David, and Mark Shapiro. *Circle of Poison: Pesticides and People in a Hungry World.* San Francisco: Institute for Food and Development Policy, 1981.

Weissman, Robert. "Replacing the Union: Business's Labor Offensive," *Multinational Monitor,* April 1991.

Welch, Kathleen A. "Democracy for Sale: The Need for Campaign Finance Reform," *In the Public Interest,* Spring 1990.

Welsh, Heidi J. "Shareholder Activism," *Multinational Monitor,* December 1988.

West, Cornel. *Race Matters.* Boston: Beacon Press, 1993.

Wolf, Naomi. *The Beauty Myth: How Images of Beauty Are Used against Women.* New York: Morrow, 1991.

World Book Encyclopedia. Chicago: World Book, 1989.

Women's Action for Nuclear Disarmament. *Mother's Day for Peace Action Kit*. Arlington, Mass.: Women's Action for Nuclear Disarmament.

Zinn, Howard. *A People's History of the United States*. New York: Harper Collins, 1980.

Zinn, Howard. *The Twentieth Century: A People's History*. New York: Harper Collins, 1984.

PERIODICALS

American Prospect. P.O. Box 383080, Cambridge, MA 02238.

Dollars and Sense. 1 Summer Street, Somerville, MA 02143.

Extra! 130 West 25th Street, New York, NY 10001.

In These Times. 2040 North Milwaukee Avenue, Chicago, IL 60647.

Left Business Observer. 250 West 85th Street, New York, NY 10024.

Mother Jones. 1663 Mission Street, San Francisco, CA 94103.

Multinational Monitor. P.O. Box 19405, Washington, DC 20036.

The Nation. 72 Fifth Avenue, New York, NY 10011.

The Progressive. 409 East Main Street, Madison, WI 53703.

Public Citizen. 2000 P Street, N.W., Suite 610, Washington, DC 20036.

The Workbook. P.O. Box 4524, Albuquerque, NM 87106.

Z Magazine. 150 West Canton Street, Boston, MA 02118.

INDEX